PHONICS AND PHONIC RESOURCES

Contents

Acknowledgements

The authors and publishers wish to express their grateful thanks to:

- Phil Bowen, John Muggeridge, Bob Parker, Pat Pomlett, Sylvia Porter, Stewart Tuft and Bob Walden for their contributions to the first edition of this handbook;
- Mr A R Payne, Headteacher of Blackheath Primary School, Rowley Regis, Sandwell for permission to reproduce test material on pages 113 to 119;
- Mr C Evans, Headteacher of Corngreaves Junior and Infant School, Cradeley Heath, Sandwell LEA for permission to print test material on pages 109 to 111;
- Phil Watts, Principal Educational Psychologist, Sandwell MBC for permission to print examples from the *Sandwell Group Phonic Test* on pages 120 to 125.

PHONICS AND PHONIC RESOURCES

Introduction

This book has been compiled following many requests from teachers for a handbook which gives practical advice on ways in which phonics can be organised and taught in the classroom.

There have been many favourable responses to the first edition since it was published in 1993, including:

> The book is essentially a resource bank of material of various kinds which will undoubtedly be of great use to schools building up their own policies and practices in this area.
> Indeed, there are few other publications around which will be as useful and NASEN is to be commended for making this book available.
>
> *(Times Educational Supplement, 28.1.94)*

Reading is the cornerstone of educational progress. Over the past 150 years, standards of reading attainment and methods of teaching reading have frequently been the subject of often heated arguments. In the 1940s and 1950s, there was polarisation between the 'whole word' (or 'look-and-say') and the 'phonic' methods. More recently, debate has focused on the merits and disadvantages of using reading schemes and 'real books'. Frequently, arguments have appeared to be centred around teachers' preferred classroom methods rather than upon childrens' particular reading requirements – at their lowest ebb, upon histrionics rather than reliable data.

The HMI Report, *The Teaching and Learning of Reading in Primary Schools* (1990), found that an exclusive concentration on any one method of reading might be associated with a higher level of failure among pupils. It concluded that the most effective teachers used a mixture of methods in the teaching of reading, and that these included the teaching of phonics.

The *National Curriculum* (1995) clearly states that, at Key Stage 1 (Key Skills), pupils should be taught to read with fluency, accuracy, understanding and enjoyment, building on what they know:

> … Pupils should be taught the alphabet, and be made aware of the sounds of spoken language in order to develop phonological awareness. They should also be taught to use various approaches to word identification and recognition, and to use their understanding of grammatical structure and the meaning of the text as a whole to make sense of print.

Recently, publishers have responded by producing a range of new phonic resources in addition to revising some 'old favourites'. Consequently, we have accepted NASEN's invitation to revise the original edition of this handbook and hope that this new edition will prove to be equally helpful in the classroom.

Mike Hinson and Pete Smith

PART I – PHONICS – ASSESSMENT AND TEACHING
Section 1 – What Do We Mean By 'Phonics'?

'Phonics' is a term used in the methodology of the teaching of reading to describe the process whereby the symbols (ie the letters) with which a word is represented in print are associated with sound values in speech. It is one of a group of decoding skills which are commonly described as *word attack skills*. The other two major ones are:

- *Configuration* – this approach to word recognition involves the child in memorising the shape and pattern of a word.
- *Context* – this relies on the child's knowledge of language and involves the identification of a less familiar word by looking at it in the context of the rest of the sentence, or a group of sentences.

    Clues, or cues, found in the grammatical construction of a sentence are known as *syntactic* clues. *Semantic* clues are discovered by interpreting the meaning of the sentence.

The teaching of phonics is beset with linguistic terminology which sometimes causes confusion. The term 'phonics' is often confused with '*phonetics*'. Phonetics is the scientific study of all speech sounds in language, and the ways in which these are produced. A special alphabet is used in phonetic notation in order to describe the sounds as they appear in any language. For example, the '1' sound in 'like' is represented as [1] and in 'feel' as [ɬ], thus indicating a slightly different positioning of the tongue when articulating the word.

Phonology is the linguistic system which deals with speech sounds in a particular language such as English. The smallest unit of sound is called a *phoneme* and there are approximately 44 in the English language. Here, the '1' sound in 'like', 'feel' and 'well' is represented phonologically as /1/. The application of phonology to the teaching of reading is termed 'phonics', particularly the association between speech sounds (phonemes) and the letters used to represent them in print (*graphemes*).

Phonics and the *National Curriculum*
The HMI Report published in 1990 revealed that, in the majority of schools, an eclectic approach to the teaching of reading is still adopted whereby the full range of basic word attack skills is incorporated in the reading programme.

At Key Stage I, the *National Curriculum* (1995) sets out the key reading skills. It expects that, within a balanced and coherent programme, pupils should be taught to use: phonic knowledge, graphic knowledge, word recognition, grammatical knowledge and contextual understanding. Phonic knowledge focuses on the relationships between print symbols and sound patterns:

Opportunities should be given for:

- recognising alliteration, sound patterns and rhyme, and relating these to patterns in letters;
- considering symbols in longer words;
- identifying initial and final sounds in words;
- identifying and using a comprehensive range of letters and sounds, including combinations of letters, blends and digraphs, and paying specific attention to their use in the formation of words;
- recognising inconsistencies in phonic patterns;
- recognising that some letters do not always produce a sound themselves but influence the sound of others.

(para. 2b)

Letters and sounds

One of the ways in which pupils can succeed in tackling and decoding unfamiliar words is by developing their understanding of *letter-sound correspondence*. When tackling a new word, a pupil must first be able to analyse it in order to determine the sounds represented, then to synthesise (or 'build up') these components in order to recognise it successfully. Studies of reading show that, for most pupils, a knowledge of phonics can help to develop reading fluency. Nevertheless, reading is a cognitive skill and no two individuals' cognitive processes follow an identical route in solving a particular problem. It follows, therefore, that in the early stages of reading, some pupils may place a greater reliance on phonics than others. Most teachers of reading can cite individual examples of, on the one hand, pupils whose reading has been boosted through the acquisition of phonic knowledge and, on the other hand, those who have become independent readers without having demonstrated any knowledge of phonics whatsoever.

The majority of teachers recognise that children make their own individual ways towards reading fluency and that it is their role to provide pupils with appropriate teaching and support at each stage of that process. It is only likely to be used effectively by a pupil once he or she has begun to correct his or her own mistakes when reading.

Certain watchwords need to be sounded. *Teaching phonics is not an end in itself*. Phonics ought not be taught in isolation but should be related to pupils' reading in a meaningful way. Overemphasis on phonic analysis and synthesis can slow down learning because it interferes with pupils' understanding of the significance of larger units of print, such as phrases and sentences. As long ago as 1975, the Bullock Report criticised the practice of encouraging children to 'build up' words by 'sounding them out' as a matter of routine. Practitioners will know that when pupils adopt the habit of looking at every letter of every word, their reading becomes hesitant and slow, almost to the point where they become more concerned with the decoding of individual words than with comprehending the ideas and meaning which they convey.

Essentially, children need to learn that letters represent sounds; that when these are put together, they make words which have a meaning; and that 'word building' is best applied to words which cannot be recognised in any other way. Once a word has been recognised and committed to memory, it is time to move on to more exciting aspects of developing fluency.

Section 2 – A Policy for the Teaching of Phonics

The HMI Report (1990) was based on 3,000 visits to primary schools. It revealed that 90 per cent of teachers taught phonics in one form or another. Of the 10 per cent who did not, most taught older classes who had already mastered these skills.

Apparently, the inspectorate found a clear link between higher standards and systematic phonic teaching. 'Phonic skills invariably formed part of the repertoire of those children who showed early success in reading.'

While the value of teaching these skills was rarely disputed, how and how often to teach phonics were 'more controversial issues' (para. 31).

It is not the intention of this teachers' handbook to enter into controversy, rather to accept that the teaching of phonics can be of benefit to the majority of pupils who are learning to read and that teachers will devise their own ways of teaching them. What can be helpful in making both learning and teaching more effective is to give access to a systematic procedure for going about things.

In order for teachers to offer positive and effective help to their pupils, a policy for teaching phonics as part of a reading policy is essential. This, in turn, will be part of a school's language policy which addresses the teaching of the four modes of language, namely listening, speaking, reading and writing, in relationship to the National Curriculum.

A five-phase approach to the initiation of a phonics policy is suggested.

Phase 1 – Policy making

Initially, it will be valuable for all members of staff to discuss phonics and the teaching of reading, then to reach a common understanding of what is involved. (As appropriate, this might necessitate some staff training from an outside source.)

Next, members of staff will need to agree upon a systematic order for the teaching of phonics. This is to ensure continuity as pupils progress from one class or group to another. Various standard works on the teaching of reading will suggest slightly different orders for teaching the different combinations of sounds. The one used in this handbook is based on the order originally suggested by Stephen Jackson in *Get Reading Right* (1971). Whichever order is finally chosen, slight variations may prove necessary and these should be made at the discretion of, and based on, the experience of the staff concerned. What *is* important is that everyone agrees to that particular order and then abides by the procedure chosen.

It is also important that all adults involved in hearing pupils read should agree on the common pronunciation of the sounds, blends and digraphs used in the early stages of reading. Local variations will need to be taken into consideration. For example, people living in the South of the country tend to use a long /a/ sound in words such as 'path' and 'bath'; those in the North are most likely to use a short /a/; while Midlanders might use either, or both, according to the locality in which they live.

Phase 2 – Setting up resources

The next joint task is to carry out a trawl of the classrooms and stock cupboards to discover what phonic resources are available. Practical experience has shown that the majority of schools already have items, including teacher-manufactured ones, that can be utilised in building up a collection of phonic resources. In these days of financial stringency, it would be unwise to proceed with the ordering of any additional materials until this stocktaking exercise has been completed.

A major section of this handbook is devoted to the classification of phonic resources and a set of criteria has been included. This should prove of particular value in assessing both items which are out of print and new ones which the staff think might be worthy of purchase. Practical ways of organising these resources for school and classroom use will be described later.

Phase 3 – Assessing pupils' knowledge of phonics

Having carried out the two preliminary phases, staff members will now be in a better position to discuss methods whereby they can ascertain pupils' varying levels of phonic knowledge.

The Attainment Targets in Reading which are part of National Curriculum English encourage hearing pupils read as a fundamental part of the learning and teaching process. One aspect of this practice is to check a pupil's progress by highlighting areas of strength and weakness. Examples of how to make the best use of such information will be given in the section on assessment. Although this information in itself might be sufficient to set up a learning programme, it can also be helpful to pinpoint more specific areas by using criterion-referenced tests (see page 9). The *Sandwell Group Phonic Tests* by John Muggeridge and Phil Bowen, published by NASEN, are good examples.

One final point: the learning of phonics depends on good speaking and listening skills. Attention to pre-reading skills in these areas may be necessary for some pupils before considering a more structured approach to the acquisition of phonic skills.

Phase 4 – Catering for individual needs

It is during this phase that teachers will marry together information about each individual's use of phonics with their own knowledge of the phonic resources available.

A major part of this handbook is concerned with the effective organisation of school and classroom resources for the teaching of phonics. Whatever system is established as the result of using this information, again it must be stressed that phonics should not become an end in themselves, some panacea for the teaching of reading. Phonics is only one element of word attack skills, and word attack skills are only part of the reading process. It is a truism to state that, in acquiring phonics as in other aspects of learning, each pupil has his or her individual needs. It will not be necessary for every pupil to complete all of the work included in the school's programme for learning phonics.

Phase 5 – Monitoring progress

Regular monitoring and recording are an essential part of ensuring that the system works effectively. The *Sandwell Group Phonics Tests*, previously mentioned, include record sheets for individual pupils and for class use. Other well-known assessment instruments such as *The Phonic Skills Tests* which are part of *Get Reading Right* by Stephen Jackson (published by Gibson) include an individual record sheet. Alternatively, and perhaps most satisfactorily, a school could design a record sheet tailored to its own particular requirements (see Appendix 1).

Regular appraisal will ensure that pupils move smoothly through their programmes, that additional practice is given as required, and that they do not linger unnecessarily on areas of phonic knowledge previously acquired and already generalised.

Section 3 – Assessing Pupils' Phonics

The assessment of pupils' progress has always featured as an important element of effective classroom practice in the teaching of reading.

Listening to a pupil read is an ideal opportunity to:

- establish a sympathetic one-to-one child–adult relationship;
- monitor progress;
- help the reader to overcome any current problems;
- praise his or her achievements.

Teacher's assessment of his or her phonic knowledge is most likely to take place during this activity. It is also probable that, for the majority, the incidental help given by the teacher is the most valuable form of instruction in the use of phonic skills because it is focused upon a tangible situation. As a result, the teacher may decide that a more detailed assessment will be necessary in order to help pupils with their phonics.

Miscue analysis

In his pioneer work, Goodman (1969) describes a method of surmising which mental processes are in operation when a person is reading. He or she is asked to read out loud a passage of continuous prose during which a careful record is kept of every response which differs from the original text. Misread words are known as 'miscues' rather than as 'errors'. (See Appendix 3.) In Goodman's view, evidence of the ways in which a reader tackles the text gives an insight into the overall strategies that he or she has utilised during the process. If these strategies appear to be ineffective, then alternatives can be suggested and demonstrated.

Readable accounts of miscue analysis are to be found in: Arnold (1982); CLPE's *The Reading Book* (1991); and the teachers' manuals of such reading schemes as *Reading 360* (Ginn).

The Running Reading Record

Described by Clay (1972, 1985), the Running Reading Record is similar in some respects to miscue analysis. However, it can be used very much more easily by teachers during day-to-day activities:

- a specially prepared text is not necessary;
- recording can be carried out on any piece of paper and without marking a prepared script;
- it can be used at any time, with any text;
- subsequent analysis is much easier.

It is advisable for teachers who wish to use it to experience some prior in-service training in a workshop situation.

In operation, a passage of at least 100 words should be chosen. The teacher then records the pupil's responses while he or she is reading. Unknown words are supplied to the reader only when this is absolutely necessary. A suggested recording key is as follows:

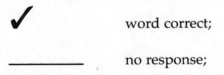

word correct;

_____ no response;

	T.A.	teacher assisted;
child:	home	substitution;
text:	here	
	n - o - t	sounding out;
	↰R	repeat of text;
	S.C.	self-correction;
child:	home	insertion.
text:	╱	

Figure 1 shows a typical passage used with a Year 2 pupil. Figure 2 is the teacher's record of the way in which Andrew dealt with this text. Although he appears to be acquiring a useful sight vocabulary in his reading, his word attack skills are not well developed. He has relied on word recognition and some recall of the traditional story.

Once upon a time
there were three bears and
they lived in the middle
of a dark wood.

The three bears had three chairs.
Father Bear had a great big chair,
Mother Bear had a middle-sized chair
and baby Bear had a little tiny chair.

The three bears had three bowls.
Father Bear had a great big bowl,
Mother Bear had a middle-sized bowl
and Baby Bear had a little tiny bowl.

The three bears had three beds.
Father Bear had a great big bed,
Mother Bear had a middle-sized bed
and Baby Bear had a little tiny bed.

Figure 1 - Sample text for Running Reading Record

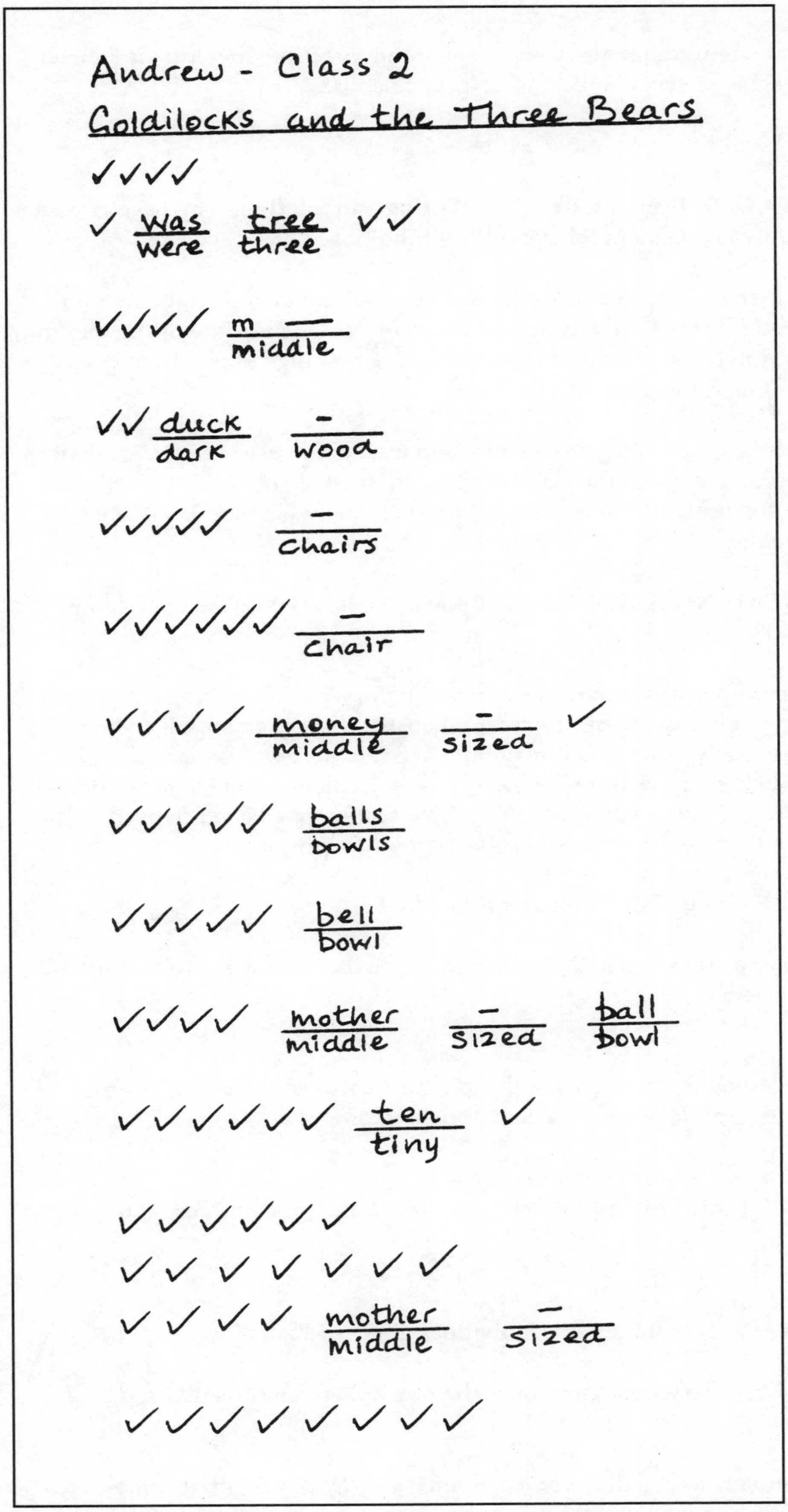

Andrew - Class 2

Goldilocks and the Three Bears.

✓✓✓✓

✓ $\frac{was}{were}$ $\frac{tree}{three}$ ✓✓

✓✓✓✓ $\frac{m}{middle}$ —

✓✓ $\frac{duck}{dark}$ $\frac{-}{wood}$

✓✓✓✓ $\frac{-}{chairs}$

✓✓✓✓✓ $\frac{-}{chair}$

✓✓✓✓ $\frac{money}{middle}$ $\frac{-}{sized}$ ✓

✓✓✓✓✓ $\frac{balls}{bowls}$

✓✓✓✓✓ $\frac{bell}{bowl}$

✓✓✓✓ $\frac{mother}{middle}$ $\frac{-}{sized}$ $\frac{ball}{bowl}$

✓✓✓✓✓✓ $\frac{ten}{tiny}$ ✓

✓✓✓✓✓
✓✓✓✓✓✓
✓✓✓✓ $\frac{mother}{middle}$ $\frac{-}{sized}$

✓✓✓✓✓✓✓

Figure 2 - Running Reading Record: responses of a Year 2 pupil

Tests of phonic knowledge

Criterion-referenced tests are now commonly used in classroom practice. They provide direct information about pupils' achievements in relation to a specified task.

The following are examples of the few published tests on the market.

ALPHA TO OMEGA: the A–Z of Teaching Reading, Writing and Spelling – by Bevé Hornsby and Frula Shear, published by Heinemann Educational (4th Edition, 1996).

The origins of this well-known programme lie in the work of Gillingham and Stillman who devised a phonetically based scheme for teaching children with specific reading difficulties in the 1930s. It has been found to be very helpful in teaching a wide range of children, young people and adults with reading difficulties.

The latest edition includes a diagnostic entry test to help teachers in placing their students at the correct level in the programme. From the point of view of assessing phonic knowledge, *Alpha to Omega* contains many sentences and passages for dictation which are invaluable in pinpointing individual weaknesses.

NEALE ANALYSIS OF READING ABILITY – by Marie D Neale. The revised version is published by NFER/Nelson (1989).

In addition to containing graded tests for the assessment of a pupil's reading progress and an analysis of reading errors and miscues, there is a comprehensive chapter on supplementary diagnostic tests. Test 1 is 'Discrimination of Initial and Final Sounds'. Test 2 is 'Names and Sounds of the Alphabet'. The tests have been devised to assist in diagnosing inconsistencies in a child's development of literacy skills, especially where low scores have been achieved in the Neale test. It is advised that they are used only 'with very young children'.

PHONIC REFERENCE FILE – by Gill Cotterell, published by LDA.

This systematic, structured approach to phonics and spelling can be used with students of all ages. There are three components:

Checklist of Basic Sounds
Intended for use with the *Diagnostic Spelling Tests*, this photocopiable checklist enables the teacher to record a continuing profile of each student's spelling progress.

Phonic Word Lists
This component consists of lists of 112 words which are indexed and graded in order of phonic difficulty.

Diagnostic Spelling Tests
These are easy-to-use, graded tests that pinpoint individual difficulties.

PHONIC SKILLS TESTS – by Stephen Jackson, published by Robert Gibson and Sons, Glasgow (1971).

The *Phonic Skills Tests* accompany a remedial scheme entitled *Get Reading Right*. It comprises a battery of 11 tests which follow an order for teaching phonemes suggested by the author, together with a record sheet.

Still in print, this scheme has stood the test of time. It is not necessary to give a child all of the tests, or even the whole of one test. The main purpose is to discover what needs to be taught. Administrators should discontinue the testing as soon as the gaps in a particular student's phonic knowledge become evident.

Tests 1 and 2 are concerned with knowledge of individual letters and can be used as a group test with an entire class. The remainder are administered individually.

SANDWELL GROUP PHONICS TESTS – by John Muggeridge and Phil Bowen (copyright Sandwell Child Psychology Service), published by NASEN (1992).

These tests have been well received by teachers. They are intended to be used with classes in Years 2 to 4, or with groups of older children who have reading difficulties. The tests are a guide to phonic awareness and help to identify children whose phonic skills:

- need further investigation through individual observation and assessment;
- are weak and for whom a structured phonic programme might be appropriate;
- are patchy and therefore need some reinforcement;
- are good and who therefore do *not* need a structured phonic programme.

The authors have recognised the difficulties inherent in presenting a group phonic test. For example, without direct one-to-one observation, the administrator cannot be sure whether or not a child is decoding, using a process of elimination, or relying on his or her knowledge of sight vocabulary. The authors also recognise that using phonics involves verbal skills, whereas the administration of group phonics tests calls for silence.

Words have been chosen to reflect spoken or receptive vocabulary rather than sight vocabulary. The distractors, or 'wrong' answers, have been chosen to represent phonic or visual alternatives.

The *Sandwell Group Phonic Tests* consist of a graded series of three tests. Phonic skills are assessed in a similar order to that of Jackson's *Phonic Skills Tests*. Test 1 should be given to a whole class or group. Children who make very few mistakes go on to Test 2. After Test 2, those children who make very few mistakes can proceed with Test 3. Results may be interpreted in the light of any patterns emerging which highlight gaps in phonic knowledge.

The package includes: a teacher's manual with examples of sentences which could be used for administering the tests; an answer sheet; and two types of record sheets.

SOUND BEGINNINGS – by Jean Gross and Julie Garnett, published by LDA, Wisbech (1996).

This pack is designed for 4–7 year-olds. It includes a method of classroom-based assessment which will enable teachers to identify those young children who would benefit from sound awareness training. In addition to a teacher's handbook, there are photocopiable sheets, two audio tapes and a set of cards. It is based on the premise that early intervention for children with poor phonological awareness is a highly efficient and effective means of preventing later reading difficulties.

SURE FIRE PHONICS – by Williams and Rogers, published by Nelson (1980).

This is a series of six books designed to introduce phonics to children in Years 3–5. Book 1 has a placement test which can be used in allocating them to the correct section of the series.

WRaPS – WORD RECOGNITION AND PHONIC SKILLS – by Clifford Carver and David Moseley (1994), Hodder and Stoughton, London.

WRaPS is especially suitable for 5–8 year-olds and can be administered either as an individual or group test. It is designed to assess children's developing word recognition and phonic skills.

The test comprises 50 items, arranged in increasing order of difficulty. Normally children are required to attempt all of the items. Each item consists of a row of words, one word of which is the correct answer. The stimulus word is given by the administrator, and the child is asked to select and underline the correct word in each row. In order to succeed, he or she must either recognise the correct spelling of the target word or must consider the alternatives, paying attention to all of their phonic elements.

A diagnostic profile is constructed from the raw data. Four types of miscue are indicated and these are interpreted as:

c – consonant grapheme incorrect;
v – vowel grapheme incorrect;
o – order of letters incorrect;
s – shortening (some letters have been omitted).

The profile has direct implications for teaching, showing whether particular attention needs to be paid to consonants, vowels, letter order or word building.

A standardised Word Recognition Age for chronological ages 5–8 can also be calculated.

Tests developed by schools

Due to the limited number of published tests, many schools have developed their own assessment instruments. In Appendices 1(a) and 1(b), there are examples from two Midlands primary schools, together with brief details of the way in which these tests are used.

Analysis and interpretation of data

This is the crucial part of assessment. Criterion-referenced tests, whether published or developed to fit the needs of an individual school, yield a wealth of information. Potential users will benefit from some in-service training. With discerning use, they will then become increasingly skilled in the interpretation of miscues and the utilisation of such information in the compilation of learning programmes designed to help children achieve progress in reading.

As an example of this process, in Appendix 2, readers can follow the progress of 'Andrew' through his attempts at Test 1 and Test 2 of the *Sandwell Group Phonics Tests*:

- In Test 1, it is evident that he has made a good start in blending two and three-letter words which contain a short vowel sound. Therefore the administrator has decided that he should be included in the test group for Test 2.
- His performance on Test 2 indicates that:
  - further reinforcement of final consonant blend will be beneficial;
  - he will need to be taught the 'magic e' rule;
  - there is confusion over initial consonant blends.

Readers might care to make a note of other aspects of his performance which may need further investigation, or areas in which he will need more help.

Armed with this data, teachers can then use the resource sections of this book in setting up a programme for Andrew, geared to his particular needs.

Section 4 – Teaching and Learning Phonics – Some Practical Considerations

The early years

Bradley (1989) demonstrated that young children develop what she termed 'phonological awareness' at an early age. She cited the work of Chunovsky who, in a seminal study (1963), had shown that rhyme-making was 'an inescapable stage in linguistic development in the second year of life'. Through rhyming, children learn to generalise from one spoken word to another. Bradley concluded that children who enter school with poor phonological skills were likely to experience difficulty in learning to read and spell. In other words, the songs, rhymes and other linguistic routines that young children so obviously enjoy both at home and at school are beneficial as informal sound practice, and as preparation for the more formal aspects of learning to read.

Spoken words are divided into two units: the *onset* which corresponds to any initial consonants, and the *rime* which corresponds to the vowel and any final consonants. Thus: *br* (onset), *ick* (rime), gives *brick*. The rime of a word such as 'pig' corresponds to the letter cluster '-ig'. Rimes may correspond to just the vowels in written words such as 'see' ('-ee'), 'too' ('-oo') and 'no' ('-o'), while words like 'ear', 'oak' and 'our' are examples of words which consist only of rimes.

The phonological skill which children can develop and bring to reading and writing is the ability to divide a word into its *onset* and *rime* and then to categorise words which have the same onset and rime. Bradley and Bryant (1985) have shown that children who are taught about alliteration and rhyming do better at reading than children who have not received this help. An awareness of rhyme alerts them to the possibility of using analogies between spelling patterns in words when they begin to read.

Goswami (1994) concludes that a good phonological foundation is required if children are to benefit from using analogies in reading. Those who start school with good rhyming and alliteration skills can be introduced to reading via analogies and word families straight away. Those with poor phonological skills will need help with rhyme and alliteration. The early stages of some recently published reading programmes incorporate materials based on developing children's phonological awareness, and others have specific materials as an integral component.

Early phonics

The acquisition of phonics is essentially an oral skill which depends for its success upon well-developed auditory discrimination. Helping young children to distinguish the difference between common domestic sounds; drawing their attention to the fact that the words which symbolise some objects begin with the same sound (bat, ball, bell); also that some words have the same ending (mug, hug, rug); and that words have different rhythms when you tap them out, are all common activities which can help to prepare pupils for a successful start to reading.

Use of phonic skills combined with good prediction of language patterns can be taught orally. There is no need for such work to be at all visual in the first instance. The teacher can produce spoken sentences which give only the initial one or two sounds of missing words, eg:

Teacher:	'The children could not [*something*] to school because of the snow,' followed by:
Teacher:	'The children could not g____ to school because of the snow.'
Pupils:	'It's "go".'

15

They should be encouraged to substitute the word 'something' for the unknown, or difficult, word, thus:

Teacher: 'The plant died because the children did not [*something*] it,'
               followed by:
Teacher: 'The plant died because the children did not w_____ it.'
Pupils: '… The children did not water it.'

Applying phonic skills when reading

It is suggested that when a pupil who is reading aloud needs help with an unknown word, he or she should be encouraged to miss out that particular word and told to actually say 'something' in its place. He or she should then be allowed to read on to the end of that phrase or sentence. Time for thinking should always be allowed before encouraging a child to make an informed guess when he or she is reading.

The passage should then be read again, either by the pupil or the teacher. Attention should be drawn to the first few sounds of the unknown word. It is also important to emphasise that the word needs to make sense in order for the phrase or sentence to make sense. Draw his or her attention to the letters and words, and letters in words, in as interesting a way as possible.

This approach encourages 'reading for meaning' and is usually more successful than instructing the reader, as a matter of course, to 'sound it out'. On some occasions, however, 'building up' the word may be the best alternative. Once a child gets the hang of such a combined phonic/reading strategy, he or she should be praised on each occasion that it is used effectively.

Introducing phonics

Especially in the early stages, when sounds are being taught for the first time, their consistent 'pure' pronunciation is essential. For this reason, many teachers prefer to teach phonics as a small group activity. Sibilant sounds, such as 's' and 'sh', fricatives such as 'f', and plosive sounds such as 't' quickly get lost across the background noise of a classroom. If children are not listening close at hand, there is always the temptation to stress the sound by adding 'uh', thus giving 'suh', 'fuh' and 'tuh'. This common practice often leads to confusion when simple blending is attempted. Many readers will remember the mystifying C-V-C (consonant-vowel-consonant) word *cuhrahtuh* which is an example of promoting such a practice. Correctly pronounced, the word represents a common domestic pet.

Teachers should also be cautious when choosing, or making their own, audio-taped materials as backup, for this reason.

Phonic resources

Although publishers have begun to introduce a wider variety of supplementary games and activities, many phonic resources currently available on the market still tend to be of the worksheet/workbook variety. Opportunities for written responses, using these or sentences evolved as a follow-up to the oral cloze-procedure exercises discussed above, are important as a reinforcement and a supplement to direct teaching.

In classroom practice, teachers will use a variety of ideas to evolve their own approaches to the teaching of phonics. However, the present writers must stress that the sole use of worksheets and/or written exercises is highly unlikely to improve children's grasp of the use of phonics as a word attack strategy. Any approach to the teaching and learning of phonics will need to be both carefully organised and proactive. A reliance on one particular series of worksheets or exercises is not advisable: simply distributing such materials and then leaving children to 'pick up' phonics on their own without direct teaching is to be positively discouraged.

Elsewhere in this book, the organisation of phonic resources is described in more detail. A method for the direct teaching of phonics, successfully developed by one teacher, is described in Section 6.

Section 5 – The Organisation of Phonic Resources

This is Phase 2 of planning and implementing a school and classroom policy for the teaching and learning of phonics.

The policy which results from staff discussions is intended to engender a consistent approach. It therefore follows that the centralisation of resources is to be recommended. Not only will this encourage the systematic use of resources by both staff and children, but it also makes good economic sense.

Location of resources

This is very much a joint decision to be taken by the members of staff in any particular school situation. The two variables which have to be reconciled are the *distance* factor and the *quantity* factor. How far will a child have to walk to the central resource base in order to borrow a particular item from the collection? For example, several smaller, strategically located resource areas rather than a single large one would be preferable in a school which has separate buildings for infants and juniors.

Adequate space for easy access will be necessary, as well as provision of shelves, storage boxes, drawers, cupboards and cabinets.

Choice of resources

Following clear guidance from the *National Curriculum* (1995), publishers have begun to produce phonic games and activities. However, schools are likely to restock gradually, as annual budgets allow.

Experience has shown that most school classrooms can yield up a variety of resources which can be utilised in some way. Fortunately, many teachers have acquired a fairly healthy 'squirrel' attitude, preserving out-of-print materials which 'might be useful' at some time in the future. Some items have been utilised continually, simply 'because they were there', others are an enduring memorial to the enthusiasm of a long-departed former colleague. The prospect of a revised system provides a welcome opportunity for a thorough sort-out and appraisal of available resources. (Hopefully, those colleagues who have built up private hoards might be persuaded to relinquish them for the common good!) For example, sets of Betty Root's *Reading Games*, formerly published by Hart-Davis, or the *Wordslides*, published by Longman, will be valuable discoveries.

However, not all out-of-print materials will prove to be as useful. A set of criteria helpful in selecting materials appears on page 30. Some of the factors that will need to be considered in the sort-out are:

- *Achieving objectives* – What is the material attempting to teach and by what methods? Is it only for 'occupying kids'?
- *Teaching order* – How will the material fit into the school's agreed order for teaching letter sounds?
- *Art work* – Some games have a long shelf life while the illustrations on, say, Stott's 'Touch Cards' are now rather dated.
- *Instructions* – Some materials can have instructions which are more complex to read than the particular phonic skills that they are designed to teach.

Setting up the resources

The next step in Phase 2 is to give due consideration as to how your varied collection of textbooks, games, work cards, worksheets and associated activities can be organised into a coherent system understood by both pupils and teachers alike.

In their classic work, *A Classroom Index of Phonic Resources* (3rd edition, 1984, published by NARE), Doris Herbert and Gareth Davies-Jones included printed pages which could be cut out. Most of this publication was devoted to the systematic listing of resources. Printed pages could be cut out and either placed in plastic wallets or stuck on to A4 pieces of card. These were then stored in a wooden box. Worksheets and work cards could also be stored there, the whole collection being colour coded. A suitable method of storing and arranging the more bulky items for easy accessibility was left to the ingenuity of its users, since it was not described in the *Index*. Overall, however, the book was a masterpiece of inventiveness.

The essence of this system was that it could be effective in utilising both teachers' time and children's motivation. In principle, a self-help element was incorporated into the over-learning elements of phonics whereby children could proceed at their own pace to find worksheets and so forth, or to play games, with an element of self-checking. Teachers' time could then be devoted to actual teaching, and to overseeing the system to ensure its smooth running. In practice, the cards did not give pupils clear guidance on which material or activity they should go on to next. Readers should bear this in mind when devising their own systems.

Phonics and Phonic Resources does not include cut-and-stick pages as it is primarily intended as a reference book. Nonetheless, some form of centralised index remains a vital part of any system for organising phonic resources. The following ideas could be considered in setting up such a resource.

- A school which already has an index based on the old NARE book could revise its cards.
- A similar system could be set up using a filing cabinet (two-drawer, rather than four-drawer, bearing in mind the height of the potential users).
- A system utilising a series of ring binders or lever-arch files could be considered. Clear plastic pockets in a variety of thicknesses are now cheaply available and colour coding can be achieved fairly easily.
- Although not quite as detailed, perhaps a 'talking' index on Language Master cards could be set up.
- All schools have access to computers. An appropriate system for gaining access to phonic resources could be devised by some staff enthusiast.

Catering for individual needs

As the result of having carried out Phase 3, the assessment of children's phonic knowledge, each child will have his or her own record sheet which summarises those skills which are already secure and those where there needs to be a learning input. As previously stressed, such a record is vital if Phase 4 (setting up an individual work schedule) and Phase 5 (monitoring progress) are to be successful.

On page 119, there is a typical example of a child's record sheet. It is relatively straightforward when dealing with one individual. Having determined a starting point, the child then moves through his or her planned programme. However, when the teacher has to deal with a class in which the majority have a variety of needs, the way forward will be influenced by several factors.

Classroom management

- How much *time* will need to be devoted to phonics? For example, if one child would benefit from a precision teaching approach, where will those few minutes per day come from?
- Will other *personnel* be available to help out from time to time, for example, part-time teachers or parents?
- What about the *geography* of the classroom? In other words, does the arrangement of the furniture lend itself to effective learning? (Recent studies have shown that certain forms of classroom arrangement can encourage or hinder concentration. See Lucas and Thomas, 1990.)

Should desks be arranged so that only two or three children can work together? Should there be areas for quiet study, for using a tape recorder or Language Master? – and so forth.

At an early stage in planning, determine:

- the number of children in the class who already have basic phonic skills and who would be usefully engaged in activities designed to extend their reading fluency;
- those children who only need revision work in certain skill areas. Often, explanation and instruction during hearing them read will be the best approach. This can be reinforced with materials from phonics resources;
- the starting point at which, initially, teacher's direct teaching will need to be focused;
- those children who will need to start at the beginning and who will probably need the most input;
- those children who may need a special approach and help in addition to what can be provided in the classroom.

The numbers involved under each heading will obviously vary according to the year group and level of reading fluency.

An intensive approach

Phonics and Phonic Resources is particularly geared to the establishment of a centralised resource which can be used as the basis of individualised phonic programmes that incorporate an element of pupil self-help. However, there are occasions where an even more determined approach might be necessary.

As an example of this, one primary school decided to implement a teaching project in order to improve the phonic attainments of pupils in Year 3.

To conclude this chapter, we include some case studies of ways in which schools have organised their approach to the teaching and learning of phonics, in the hope that they will be a source of information, inspiration even, for other classroom practitioners.

Study A – Infant and Junior School

The school draws on a mixed catchment area. Some of the pupils enter the school having attended the local nursery but for a large majority of the intake the Reception class is their first experience of an educational setting.

The school has recently introduced a baseline profile which identifies early skills in basic literacy and numeracy. This provides a value added measure when reapplied at the end of Year R.

There is also an ongoing Reading Profile for Key Stage 1, Key Stage 2 (Special Educational Needs) and one for Key Stage 2 pupils who do not have special educational needs.

The profile includes sight word recognition – common words and core sight words for the reading schemes used, and a record of phonic skills including phonological awareness and specific difficulties.

Pupils in Reception start learning to read using *One, Two, Three and Away*. The full range of support materials are available and used in a well-structured way. Early phonic skills are introduced using *Letterland* but once the pupils have progressed beyond letter sounds a wide variety of resources available in a central resource are used for small groups of pupils at the same level of phonic awareness.

During Key Stage 1 pupils who have made good progress on *One, Two, Three and Away*, and who have developed a foundation of phonic skills, are moved off the scheme and use supplementary reading books arranged in readability levels. Structure phonic work through a hierarchy of skills until the pupil has mastered the more common vowel digraphs.

Pupils still in need of a structured scheme after finishing Key Stage 1 are placed on the *Fuzzbuzz* scheme. The full range of supplementary resources are available from the school Special Educational Needs Co-ordinator (SENCO) and used with all pupils. Progress is closely monitored and details entered in the Reading Profile. The phonic materials for the scheme are used with all pupils but are introduced earlier than suggested by the publishers to ease the transition to Level 2 of the scheme The *Fuzzbuzz* phonic materials are supplemented by a wide range of other published materials available from a central resource.

The school has a home-school liaison system which supports reading at home. This can include worksheet-based activities to consolidate phonic skills taught within the school.

The approach of moving pupils off a structured scheme when they have made good progress instead of placing them on a scheme after they have failed to make progress seems to work but the system has not been in place long enough for a full evaluation. It has already become clear, however, that placing an emphasis on the early acquisition of phonic skills has had a beneficial effect upon the pupils' progress.

Study B – Secondary School

The school has a high proportion of pupils with an ethnic minority background. A significant number of pupils enroll at the school with very little spoken English. The school benefits from the support of two full-time teachers from the Ethnic Minorities Support Service.

The school receives reading test scores for all pupils transferring from the local education authority feeder primary schools. These scores are used to identify pupils needing to be entered onto the Special Needs Register at Stages 1, 2 or 3.

Those placed on Stage 3 follow a reading programme based upon *Wellington Square*. The full range of support materials for the scheme are available in the suite of rooms set aside for special needs.

Support staff provide withdrawal group teaching for 30 minutes several days each week at the start of the morning. These groups are available for Year 7 and Year 8 pupils, with each member of staff helping three or four pupils.

Further support is provided by a peer tutoring system which pairs off each pupil with a proficient reader.

Phonics are taught using the support materials which are part of the *Wellington Square* scheme. This is supplemented where necessary with other materials from a variety of publishers. Dual language materials for early phonic skills are used with pupils with limited knowledge of English. These pupils are paired off with pupils speaking their mother tongue but who are also proficient in spoken English in order to provide help throughout the school day.

Group reading tests are administered to the pupils in withdrawal groups twice each year to monitor progress, evaluate the programme and identify any pupils who need to move towards formal assessment procedures.

Given the number of pupils starting at the school with significant difficulties in reading, very few are considered for formal assessment at the end of two years using the withdrawal programme, suggesting that the system used for support in Years 7 and 8 is effective.

Section 6 – Suggestions for the Direct Teaching of Phonics

From time to time, in various publications concerned with the teaching of reading and learning difficulties, some classroom practitioners enthusiastically describe their own particular methods for teaching phonics. Some might even infer that they have developed *the* ideal way of going about things.

No such claim is made for the following technique, developed by Sylvia Porter, which has been used successfully to help many children with reading difficulties.

Getting started
- Arrange the children in a semi-circle around the board. Tell them what you are going to do and why you are doing it.
- Have the child with the most marked difficulties placed centrally so that you can maintain good eye contact.
- Encourage the children to watch your *finger* and not your face as you point towards individual letters or words.
- Develop a technique which is designed to give each child *thinking time*. Never actually touch the blackboard unless you want a vocal response as a consequence.
- Always begin anything new by *modelling* – that is, by showing the children the right way, by doing it yourself first. Try to revert to this if any child makes a mistake, rather than saying, 'No! That's wrong!'

Teaching initial letters
Having assembled your group of no more than ten in a semi-circle, or two semi-circles, around the blackboard, write the following letters on the board, spacing them well apart:

b   f   s

m   a

Then you say:
    'It's my turn – when I touch it, I'll say it. I'll keep on saying it as long as I touch it.'

Then, point underneath a letter (*do not touch the board yet*). Move your hand directly away from the board, saying:
    'Get ready!'

Then, dramatically touch the board under the same letter –
- for approximately *two seconds* if a long sound is required, such as '…mmm…', or
- spring *directly off* if a quick sound such as 'd' is needed.

Meanwhile, say the correct sound yourself. Then say:
    'It's your turn (meaning the group). When I touch it, you say it. Keep on saying it as long as I touch it.'

Then again, point to underneath the same letter (not actually touching the board) and move your hand directly away from the board, saying:
    'Get ready!'

Then, directly zoom in and touch underneath the letter for the appropriate length of time – and the group should respond. If they do not, or someone gets it wrong, *model it the correct way*, beginning with:

'It's my turn…'

and repeat the whole procedure. Try not to say, 'No! That's wrong!', but always praise anyone doing exactly what is required.

This technique can then be applied for each letter. Initially, it is always better to give turns to the whole group together, thus giving the children confidence. After this, individuals can be given turns. Let those who have been quickest on the uptake perform first, thus providing additional models for the others.

It is quite possible to teach the letters for more than one of the objectives at the same time. Simply enclose each set of letters in circles and write names by the appropriate circle.

Teaching blending
Say it fast (Stage One)
This activity is aimed at teaching children to listen very carefully and to synthesise sounds in words. At first, it should be carried out entirely *orally*, with no reference at all to written symbols.

With the children gathered round you in a semi-circle, say:
'I am going to say something *very* slowly. When I give you the signal, see if you can say it the fast way.'

Get the group's complete attention. This can be more easily achieved if you develop a *watching signal*, such as holding up your hand (level with your face), palm facing the group. They should be watching you. Praise any child who gives you his or her complete attention.

With your hand raised in the watching signal position, say something very slowly, such as:
'Iiiissss-crreeem!'
Then say:
'Say it fast!' – lower your hand, thus giving the signal for their response.
The children should respond with:
'Ice-cream' – said at the normal pace.
If they do not, you model the correct way by saying:
'It's my turn,' and repeat the procedure yourself.
Again, *get complete attention*. Praise good behaviour.
You say:
'It's my turn. Listen! Iiisss-crreeem!' and then say it normally:
'Ice-cream.'

This activity should be repeated as often as needed using words which contain two, three or four syllables until you feel confident that each individual child is listening and understands how to respond to the signal, 'Say it fast!'

Blending (Stage Two)
This can be started as a group or individual activity as soon as children have successfully learned ten of the letter sounds. In other words, they have shown by the use of probe sheets such as Sheet 1, the example on page 130, that they can say the sounds made by 38 out of 40 examples on two consecutive occasions.

It is essential that only those symbols are used, as there must be no guessing at this stage.

If 'b', 'f', 's', 'm', 'a' and 't', 'c', 'h', 'r', 'e' are the symbols, write a series of words on the blackboard such as:

.Sam	.set
.rat	.hem
.mat	.met

The dot emphasises the need to start on the left. It also gives children *thinking time*.

Your finger should pause on the dot before you begin to read or sound out.

You then begin to loop your finger to touch, and pause, underneath the letter in the word, simultaneously saying the sounds as you touch them. Because some of the sounds are long ones, in effect, you almost 'sing' the words. This makes blending easier for children who have auditory weaknesses.

Immediately after sounding out a word, you return your finger to the first letter and move it quickly underneath that word as you read it the 'fast' way, in other words at a normal pace.

You then say:
'It's your turn. When I touch it, you say it. Keep on saying it as long as I touch it. Sound it out! Get ready!' (Touch the dot.)

Then, start looping as before, touching underneath each letter, and so forth. When the last letter has been sounded out, you say:
'Say it fast!' – repeat the quick movement of your finger beneath the word from left to right.

This procedure should produce the required results. If it does not, then model it the correct way again. Hopefully, you can then give turns to 'sound out' and 'say it fast', first of all to the group and then to individuals.

This method can be followed whenever a word can be phonically blended. Children find it very helpful if you continue to use the same wording and finger movements if they come to an unknown word while reading aloud to you.

Recording and monitoring progress
If possible, involve the children in recording their own progress. They need to be made aware that they need to 'pass' each set target on two consecutive occasions. They should also be encouraged to improve on their previous recorded result. In other words, they are competing against themselves.

As stated previously, the criterion for passing is that each child should say 38 out of 40 sounds on two consecutive occasions.

Each child should be tested at least *three times per week*. Each test should be dated, with the actual errors being noted. Parental involvement can be of outstanding help here.

Each success, and number of successes, should be emphasised to the child. Praise should be given as each target is passed.

Section 7 – Glossary

alliteration	–	words beginning with the same letter or sound.
analogy	–	using one word as the basis for working out the pronunciation or spelling of another word with the same rhyme, eg 'wet' – net, get, set.
analysis	–	as applied to phonics, the breaking down of a word into its individual phonemes.
auditory discrimination	–	the ability to detect differences and similarities in sound images.
blending	–	the process of linking together the constituent sounds of a word to make a whole word.
consonant blends	–	a combination of two or three consonants, blended in such a way that each letter in the blend retains its own identity, eg sl, cl, str, scr.
decoding	–	graphemes are decoded into phonemes, ie groups of letters are given their sounds in reading.
digraph	–	a combination of two letters to make a single sound: Consonant digraphs – sh, ch, wh, th, ph, ck. Vowel digraphs – oy, ay, aw, ar, ir, or, ew.
diphthong	–	two adjacent vowels which represent one vowel sound: oi, ee, ie ei, ai.
double consonants	–	eg ll, ff, ss, zz, ck.
dyslexia	–	a specific learning difficulty (SpLD). A term used to indicate a person's particular learning problems in reading, writing and spelling which do not respond to normal teaching and which might be due to minimal brain damage or impairment of neural mechanisms.
encoding	–	phonemes are encoded into graphemes, ie the sounds we hear and speak are represented in writing or printing by groups of letters.
grapheme	–	the written form of a letter.
'magic' e	–	a term used to describe the lengthening of a vowel sound in a word of one syllable by adding an 'e' after the final consonant. The medial vowel then 'says its own name', eg fate, cake, like.
miscue analysis	–	a procedure for analysing what children do as they read a text aloud. It involves the recording and evaluation of mistakes or errors as an indication as to the success of the reader's decoding strategies.
onset	–	the beginning sound of a word, eg *st* in 'stop'; *th* in 'thing'; or a syllable in a multi-syllabic word, eg *scarecrow*.

phoneme	– the smallest unit of sound that changes the meaning of a word. There are about 44 in the English language.
phonetics	– the scientific study of all speech sounds in language and the ways in which these are produced.
phonics	– the application of phonology to the teaching of reading. Emphasis is placed on sound values as a means of word recognition.
phonological awareness	– the ability to recognise and manipulate shared sounds in words.
pictogram	– a device used whereby a picture represents an object, thought or incident.
precision teaching	– this focuses on the procedures required to monitor performance in order to provide the teacher with feedback on the effectiveness of his or her instruction. Precision teaching permits the daily monitoring of a child's progress when receiving instruction on a specific skill.
prefix	– a verbal element placed at the beginning of a word to qualify its meaning, eg ab-, dis-, sub-.
rime	– that part of a word which rhymes with another word. The sound corresponding to the remaining letters of a syllable, eg '-ip' in zip, drip, strip and turnip.
suffix	– a verbal element placed at the end of a word to modify its meaning, eg -ful, -ly, -ous.
synthesis	– as applied to phonics, the joining of constituent sounds to make a complete word.
visual discrimination	– the ability to discriminate differences and similarities in shape, size and colour.
word building	– the process of building up a word from its constituent sounds.

Section 8 – References

Arnold, H (1982) *Listening to Children Read*. Hodder and Stoughton: Sevenoaks.

Barrs, M and Thomas, A (eds) (1991) *The Reading Book*. Centre for Language in the Primary School (CLPE), Webber Row, London SE1 8QW.

Bradley, L (1989) 'Predicting Learning Disabilities' in J J Dumont and H Nakken (eds) *Learning Disabilities*, Volume 2. Swets and Zeitlinger: Amsterdam.

Bradley, L and Bryant, P E (1985) *Children's Reading Problems*. Blackwell: Oxford.

Chukovsky, K (1963) *From two to five*. University of California Press: Berkeley and Los Angeles.

Clay, M (1989) 'Observing Young Children Reading Texts', *Support for Learning* Vol. 4, No. 1.

DES (1975) *A Language for Life* (The Bullock Report). HMSO.

DES (1990) *The Teaching and Learning of Reading*.

DfEE (1995) *The National Curriculum*. HMSO.

Goodman, K (1969) 'Analysis of oral reading miscues: applied psycholinguistics', *Reading Research Quarterly*, 1, 3.

Goodman, Y and Burke, C (1972) *Reading Miscue Inventory*. Macmillan: New York.

Goswami, U (1994) 'The role of analogies in reading development', *Support for Learning*, Vol. 9, No. 1.

Goswami, U (1996) *Rhyme and Analogy*, Teacher's Guide. Oxford University Press: Oxford.

Herbert, D and Davies-Jones, G (1982) *A Classroom Index of Phonic Resources*. NARE: Stafford.

Jackson, S (1971) *Get Reading Right*. Gibson: Glasgow.

Lucas, D and Thomas, G (1990) 'The Geography of Classroom Learning', *British Journal of Special Education*, 17, 1.

Muggeridge, J and Bowen, P (1992) *Sandwell Group Phonic Tests*. NASEN Enterprises: Tamworth.

PART II – PHONIC RESOURCES

Introduction

Part II is concerned with the effective organisation of school and classroom resources for the teaching of phonics.

In Section 9, readers will find a set of criteria for the evaluation of resource items. These should prove helpful not only when inspecting samples of new materials prior to purchase but also when evaluating the potential of existing items in the school's collection of phonic resources.

Section 10 is a checklist of resources currently available from publishers. It includes brief details of workbooks, worksheets, work cards, photocopy masters, textbooks and resource books. A contact address and telephone number accompanies the first mention of each publisher.

Many reading schemes and programmes include phonics as an integral part of their content. Some of these items can be used in conjunction with other resources; some are most effective only when used as part of the schemes for which they were intended. Section 11 gives concise details.

Section 12 is devoted to an index of resource materials. Most of them have already been described in previous sections. In addition, some widely used series, now out of print, have also been included and these are marked (O/P). The index has been organised according to a widely accepted order for teaching the elements of phonics. Readers will be able to see at a glance what is available and where to find it. The materials included in Section 12 are likely to form the foundation of many schools' resource collections.

Section 13 consists of an annotated list of games and activities currently available. A much wider range has made its appearance recently, providing a 'fun' element to learning and valuable reinforcement for children which they can often use on a self-help basis.

Computer software for teaching and learning phonics is a burgeoning market. The lists included in Section 14 will serve as an introduction for readers. However, we conclude that 'hands-on' experience is the most effective way of evaluating these programs. Assistance is often available from centres and advisers within local education authorities.

Finally, the word lists in Section 15 are intended as a quick reference for teaching or producing home-made materials.

The authors have been assisted in the compiling of these sections by positive comments and suggestions from users of the first edition of this handbook.

Section 9 – Criteria for the Evaluation of Phonic Resources

With publishers producing a diversity of phonic resources, deciding which ones to use can present problems. The following criteria provide a structure for looking at materials more objectively. They will act as a guide when ordering new materials; also in the evaluation of items which already form part of the school's resource collection.

Descriptive
What is the format of the material?
a) textbook?
b) workbook?
c) work cards?
d) worksheets?
e) games?
f) software?
g) auditory – audio tapes?
h) auditory – visual – eg Language Master?

Evaluative
1. *Are the following appropriate for intended purpose and pupils?*
a) layout?
b) illustrations (if any)?
c) size and type?
d) durability?
e) comprehension levels?

2. *Are the materials:*
a) attractive and stimulating?
b) carefully graded?
c) value for money?
d) Do they have a sufficient variety of content?
e) Are illustrations and text up to date?

3. *How suitable are the materials for:*
a) individual use?
b) group use?
c) Infant-aged pupils?
d) Junior-aged pupils?
e) Secondary-aged pupils?

4. *Are the materials useful for:*
a) teaching a particular skill?
b) reinforcement and consolidation?

5. *Will the materials require:*
a) additional storage facilities?
b) duplicating facilities?
c) photocopying?
d) changes in classroom organisation?

6. *Do the materials have:*
a) a teacher's manual?
b) a set of notes?

7. *Are the instructions easy to understand by:*
a) pupils?
b) an individual child?
c) teachers?
d) parents?
e) other assistants?

8. *Could parents use the materials as part of supporting classwork?*

9. *Does the material actually teach what it aims to teach?*

10. *Are there any obvious gaps?*

11. *What degree of teacher support is needed?*

Section 10 – Checklist of Resources

This is an annotated list of materials currently available from publishers. It includes the series of photocopy masters, workbooks, worksheets and resource books which form the basis of Section 11.

Active Phonic Workbooks
(Ginn and Company, Prebendal House, Parsons Fee, Aylesbury HP20 2QY Tel: 01296 88411)
Consumable workbooks covering phonic skills from letter sounds to letter strings and early phonic rules. They include both capital and lower-case letters. Activities include picture-word matching and correct letter formation. A *Teacher's Resource Book* with further suggestions and 60 photocopy masters is also available.

All Aboard – Pattern and Rhyme Workbooks
(Ginn and Company)
Consumable workbooks (30 pages) in A4 format designed for use in conjunction with the *Pattern and Rhyme* reading books. Phonic skills are developed through activities which include word-picture matching and correct letter formation. Suitable for Key Stages 1 and 2.

Alpha to Omega Activity Pack 1
(Heinemann Educational, School Orders Dept, Freepost, PO Box 381, Oxford 0X2 8BR Tel: 01865 314333)
Spirally bound, photocopiable worksheets in A4 format provide a multi-sensory approach which is especially helpful to pupils who have specific learning difficulties (SpLD). Well structured with a range of activities. Suitable from Key Stage 1 onwards.

'bdpq' Reading and Writing Book
(Kickstart Publications Ltd, 38 Awbridge Road, Netherton, Dudley, West Midlands DY2 0JA Tel: 01384 258535)
Spirally bound, photocopiable worksheets in A4 format (70+ pages). Includes a comprehensive resource with wide-ranging activities for the correction of b/d and p/q confusion. Suitable for Key Stages 1 and 2.

The Big Book of Early Phonics
(Prim-Ed Publishing, PO Box 051, Nuneaton CV11 6ZU Tel: 01203 352002)
Fifty A4 pages of copy masters designed to assist teachers with the introduction of initial letter sounds. Suitable for Key Stages 1 and 2.

Breaking the Code
(Learning Materials Ltd, Dixon Street, Wolverhampton WV2 2BX Tel: 01902 54026)
Ten photocopiable worksheets in A4 format, comb-bound. Each page presents a series of letters with corresponding numbers. The pupil writes words by writing down letters which correspond to a set of numbers. Each page focuses on a particular phonic element. Suitable for Key Stages 1 and 2.

Cloze and Phonic Activities 1–8
(Hilda King Educational Services, Ashwells Manor Drive, Penn, Buckinghamshire HP10 8EU Tel: 01494 817947)
Photocopiable A4 worksheets (30+ pages), comb-bound. Audiotapes are available. Activities include cloze stories and sentences, word sums and identification of words with the relevant phonic element. Pages are clearly laid out and amusing illustrations are included. Suitable for Key Stages 1 and 2.

The Consonant Digraph Book

(Kickstart Publications Ltd)

Sixty-plus A4 photocopiable worksheets, spirally bound. The wide range of activities includes crosswords, word-picture matching, cloze procedure, and building words with cut-and-stick. Suitable for Key Stages 1 and 2.

Crosswords

(Hilda King Educational Services)

Photocopiable worksheets (15+ pages) in A4 format, comb-bound. Each crossword addresses one phonic element. Clues are well suited to the Key Stages 1 and 2 target group. Supplementary questions provide further writing activities.

Finger Phonics

(Jolly Learning Ltd, Clare Hall, Chapel Lane, Chigwell, Essex 1G7 6JJ Tel: 0181 501 0405)
(also available from LDA)

Seven books, made from stiff cardboard, cover the 40+ sounds of English. Grooved letter shapes on each page guide the pupils to trace the correct formation of letters. There are activities for each sound and the series complements *The Phonics Handbook* by Sue Lloyd (from the same publisher). Suitable for Key Stage 1 or earlier.

The First Phonic Blending Book

(Kickstart Publications Ltd)

Photocopiable worksheets (80+ pages) in A4 format, spirally bound. Provides a tightly structured series of activities which progress from C-V blending, V-C blending to C-V-C blending with five vowels. Includes rhyming activities and checklists. Suitable for Key Stage 1 and upwards.

First Vowel Digraph Book

(Kickstart Publications Ltd)

Photocopiable worksheets (60+ pages) in A4 format, spirally bound. Activities include word searches, crosswords, cut-and-stick picture-word matching and cloze procedure. Several worksheets are dedicated to each digraph. Revision exercises and supplementary activities are included. Suitable for Key Stage 2 and upwards.

Flying Boot

(Thomas Nelson and Sons Ltd, Customer Services, ITPS Ltd, North Way, Andover, Hampshire SP10 5BE Tel: 01264 342992)

The Big Sound and Rhythm Book

For use in conjunction with the 'Sound and Rhyme' cassette tape. A large book with colour illustrations designed for group work. Suitable for Key Stage 1 or earlier.

Phonic Workbooks

Consumable workbooks for use in conjunction with the phonic-based reading books in this reading scheme. There is a strong emphasis on phonological awareness. Supported by an interactive CD-ROM and photocopy masters. Suitable for Key Stages 1 and 2.

Fuzzbuzz Workbooks

(Oxford University Press, Educational Division, Walton Street, Oxford OX2 6DP Tel: 01865 56767)
See page 40 for details.

Ginn Phonic Workbooks 1–6

(Ginn and Company)

Large-format books that give systematic practice in all the main letter sounds and blends. Have withstood the test of time.

Helper Books

(Learning Materials Ltd)

Book 3 (Letter b); Book 4 (Letter p); Book 5 (Letter d). Consumable workbooks (15+ pages) in A4 format. Activities include tracing over letters with correct pencil travel, cut-and-stick, sound-picture matching, and word completion. Suitable for Key Stages 1 and 2.

Key Phonics

(Collins Educational, Harper Collins Publishers, Freepost (GW5078), Westerhill Road, Bishopbriggs, Glasgow G64 1BR)

Four consumable A4 workbooks. Activities consist mainly of word-picture matching and simple cloze procedure exercises. At Level 1, there is a set of 50 copy masters to teach the shape and sound of consonants and vowels.

Language 1

(Longman Group Ltd, Customer Services, Freepost, Pinnacles, Harlow CM19 4BR
Tel: 01279 623921)

Teacher's Resource Book

A4 spirally bound (200 pages). Contains suggestions for a multi-sensory approach to early language skills including phonics. Covers letter sounds to common digraphs. Suitable for Key Stages 1 and 2.

Language 1 Activity Books

Three large format picture books which introduce phonic skills from letter sounds to common digraphs.

Language 1 Alphabet Cards

These laminated, A5 cards each present a letter on one side and a matching picture on the reverse. Black printed on white.

Language 1 Copymasters

A set of 100 A4 copy masters to support the *Teacher's Resource Book*. Provides a range of activities for the development of phonic skills linked with handwriting and spelling skills.

Learning Phonics 1 and 2

(Hilda King Educational Services)

Learning Phonics 1

This kit comprises six audiotapes with supporting A4 photocopiable worksheets. The following sounds, digraphs and blends are covered: l, -ell, -ill, -all, -ight (Tape 1); -ang, -ing, -ong, -ung (2); ee, oo, ai, oa (3); sh, st, ch, sp (4); ar, ir, th, -age (5); -ace, -ice, -ale, -ile.

Learning Phonics 2

Six audiotapes and supporting worksheets to cover: short vowels (1); br, cr, dr, pr (2); dl, cl, sc, sw (3); aw, ew, ay, oi (4); ea, ou, th, wh (5); mp, nd, nk, ck (6).

The Letter Sound Book

(Kickstart Publications Ltd)

Photocopiable worksheets (90+ pages) in A4 format, spirally bound. Activities include pencil travel, matching, crosswords, and cut-and-stick activities. Suitable for Key Stages 1 and 2.

The Magic 'e' Book

(Kickstart Publications Ltd)

Photocopiable worksheets in A4 format (60+ pages), spirally bound. Well-structured activities including word-picture matching, cloze procedure, crosswords and word searches. Plenty of practice is provided for each vowel sound. Revision exercises and supplementary activities are included. Suitable for Key Stages 1 and 2.

My Alphabet Fold-a-Book

(Prim-Ed Publishing)

Photocopiable sheets which introduce each letter of the alphabet with accompanying activities. On completion, pages are folded into a small book.

New Phonic Blending

(Learning Materials Ltd)

Photocopiable A4 worksheets, comb-bound. Audiotapes are an integral part of the kit. Groups of initial, medial and final sounds are provided and the pupil uses these to make words which are then inserted in sentences. Further activities help to develop auditory discrimination. Suitable for Key Stages 1 and 2.

Oxford Junior Workbooks 1–8

(Oxford University Press)

Consumable workbooks (48 pages) in A4 format. There is a wide variety of activities, some of which are designed to develop early phonic skills. Suitable for Key Stages 1 and 2.

Oxford Reading Tree – Woodpecker Workbooks

(Oxford University Press)

The *Woodpeckers* 'branch' supports work on developing phonic skills as an integral part of this reading programme. There are two series of workbooks, A–E and 1–9. Activities involve writing over a dotted word to make a key word, sentence completion, letter-letter matching and creating new words. There is a *Teacher's Guide* which contains photocopiable materials.

Phonic Blending

(Learning Materials Ltd)

Original version of *New Phonic Blending* described above. Still viable.

Phonic Crosspatches

(Prim-Ed Publishing)

Books 1–3 of A4 photocopiable sheets reinforce the learning of phonics. Graded in difficulty through to multi-syllabic words.

Phonic Fold-Ups

(Prim-Ed Publishing)

Books 1–3 of A4 photocopiable pages deal with phonic blends. Pages fold up to make a small book on completion.

Phonic Ladders

(Easylearn, Trent House, Fiskerton, Southall, Nottinghamshire NG25 0UH Tel: 01636 830240)

Photocopiable worksheets in A4 format, spirally bound (30+ pages). Pupils develop vertical lists of words with common letter strings which focus on a particular phonic element. As well as developing phonic skills and promoting phonological awareness, this resource helps to develop pupils' awareness of spelling patterns. Suitable for Key Stages 1 and 2.

Phonic-Links

(Collins)

Three packs of copy masters A4 format, spirally bound. *Phonic-Links 1* suggests activities to develop awareness of speech sounds and concepts about print. *Phonic-Links 2* and *3* tackle single letters and the main letter groupings. Suitable for Key Stage 1 and upwards.

Phonic Rhyme Time
(Robinswood Press, South Avenue, Stourbridge, West Midlands DY8 3XY)
A collection of 200 or so phonic rhymes for precise practice in speaking and reading. Memorable rhymes which focus on exact sounds. Suitable for Key Stage 2 and upwards.

Phonic Worksheets
(Prim-Ed Publishing)
Books 1–3 of A4 photocopiable worksheets motivate young pupils by incorporating their inherent love of rhyming language with the learning of phonics. Categorised in word family groupings.

Phonics Activities Resource Bank
(Stanley Thornes Publishers Ltd, Customer Services Dept, Ellenborough House, Wellington Street, Cheltenham GL50 1YW Tel: 01242 577944)
Contains 140 photocopiable pages of puzzles, race games, jigsaws and dominoes which cover all the key sounds. For use on its own or to support *The Phonics Book*, described above.

The Phonics Bank
(Ginn and Company)
Four sets of durable cards (51 cards per set) in a storage box. Phonic skills range from letter sounds to diphthongs and silent letters. An audio cassette tape is included, also a *Teacher's Resource Book*. Suitable for Key Stage 1 and upwards.

The Phonics Book
(Stanley Thornes)
Contains 116 copy masters in A4 format, spirally bound. The activities for letter sounds consist largely of copying each letter with correct pencil travel. Vowel digraphs and diphthongs are not covered in sufficient depth to teach each element, but the worksheets could be useful as a source of supplementary material. Suitable for Key Stages 1 and 2.

Phonics Books 1–9
(Easylearn)
Photocopiable worksheets in A4 format, spirally bound. Activities mainly consist of word-picture matching, often in multi-choice form. Drawing activities are also included. Suitable for Key Stage 1 and Key Stage 2.

The Phonics Handbook
(Jolly Learning Ltd)
Includes photocopiable A4 worksheets, spirally bound. Worksheets concerned with letter sounds mainly consist of copying activities designed to promote correct pencil travel. There is a good selection of supplementary activities to promote phonological awareness. Suitable for Key Stages 1 and 2.

Read, Write and Spell
(Heinemann)
Four consumable A4 workbooks intended for pupils with significant general learning difficulties in the basic language skills. Activities range from sound-picture matching to cloze procedure with more advanced phonic skills. Suitable for Key Stages 1 and 2.

Rhyme and Analogy
(Oxford University Press)
Alphabet Frieze – shows 26 letters of the alphabet and four digraphs.
Tabletop Alphabet Pack – initial sounds and letter shapes.
Alphabet Photocopy Masters – practice for initial sounds and shapes, and letter formation.
Story Rhyme Photocopy Masters – photocopiable worksheets (128 pages) in A4 format, spirally bound. Provide a range of activities for developing phonological awareness. Key Stages 1 and 2 (see also page 86).

The Second Letter Sound Book
(Kickstart Publications Ltd)
Supplement to *The Letter Sound Book*. Provides further activities to teach 26 letter sounds. Suitable for Key Stages 1 and 2.

The Second Phonic Blending Book
(Kickstart Publications Ltd)
Photocopiable worksheets, A4 format, spirally bound. Provides a tightly structured series of activities to teach initial and final consonant blends which progress to C-C-V-C, C-V-C-C and C-C-V-C-C blending. Includes supplementary activities and checklists. Suitable for Key Stage 1 and upwards.

The Second Vowel Digraph Book
(Kickstart Publications Ltd)
Photocopiable worksheets, A4 format, spirally bound. A range of activities to cover each digraph in depth. Revision exercises and supplementary activities are included. Suitable for Key Stage 2 and upwards.

Sound Practice, 1–5
(Schofield and Sims Ltd, Dogley Mill, Fenay Bridge, Huddersfield HD8 0NQ Tel: 01484 607080)
Five books offering structured phonic practice. The series begins with initial sounds, progresses through end sounds, medial sounds, initial blends and double vowel sounds.

Sounds Alive
(Belair Publications Ltd, PO Box 12, Twickenham TW1 1NR Tel: 0181 8926383)
Photocopiable A4 worksheets, wire bound (60+ pages). Divides letter sounds into voiced and unvoiced sets, with a separate set for vowel sounds. Includes characters, poems and stories to reinforce letter sound knowledge. Suitable for Key Stage 1.

Sounds Easy
(Egon Publishers Ltd, Royston Road, Baldock, Hertfordshire SG7 6NW Tel: 01462 894498)
Seventeen reading books each dedicated to providing practice for a specific phonic element. Each book is supported by A4 photocopiable worksheets in two wire-bound books (50+ pages). These use simple comprehension exercises to reinforce the phonic skill. Suitable for Key Stage 1.

Sounds, Patterns and Words
(Collins)
Four 32-page workbooks which analyse sounds. Ninety-two patterns are covered. Each page concentrates on a single letter and its sound and a revision section concludes each book. For Key Stage 1 upwards.

Soundstart
(Stanley Thornes)
Phonics Workshop 1 is a complete graduated phonics resource which introduces the 26 initial letter and five medial vowel sounds. It comprises a *Teacher's Guide*; 31 A4 focus cards; one copy of each of the ten *Soundstart 1* storybooks; three posters and a frieze; games; and an audio cassette. There is also a set of Language Master cards which provide additional practice.
Phonics Workshop 2 is a structured resource for teaching phonics at Key Stages 1 and 2 (P3–P7 in Scotland). It focuses on initial and final blends; double consonants; and consonant and vowel digraphs. The progression is very gradual. The workshop consists of a *Teacher's Guide*; 80 four-page focus cards; one copy each of the *Soundstart 2* storybooks; three posters and a frieze; games; an audio cassette; and computer software.

SpLD Phonic Skills Books 1 and 2
(Kickstart Publications Ltd)
Photocopiable worksheets in A4 format, wire bound (60 pages). These provide a variety of activities designed to match the needs and interests of pupils with specific learning difficulties. Suitable for Key Stage 2 and above.

SRA Schoolhouse Word Skills 1
(McGraw-Hill Book Company, Shoppenhangers Road, Maidenhead, Berkshire SL6 2QL
Tel: 01628 770224)
Topics covered include consonants, consonant combinations, vowels, vowel consonant patterns, compound words, contractions and endings. Each of the nine levels concentrates on a single word attack skill but also includes reinforcement of preceding skills. Previously marketed as *Schoolhouse Word Attack Skills 1*. The kit includes 340 colour-coded exercise cards, overlays, markers, a teacher's guide and a pupils' progress chart.

Stile Early Phonics
(LDA, Duke Street, Wisbech, Cambridgeshire Tel: 01945 63441)
Comprises 32 A4 cards illustrated in full colour. These cover all letter sounds, progressing from letter-letter matching to letter-picture matching in a wide variety of contexts. Suitable for Key Stages 1 and 2.

Stile Phonic Practice Cards
(LDA)
Thirty-two full colour durable A4 cards covering phonic skills ranging from short vowel sounds to common letter clusters. The pupil chooses the correct phonic element to match the pictures. Suitable for Key Stages 1 and 2.

Supersonics
(Ginn and Company)
Twenty-four phonic readers which, the publishers claim, can be used alongside any reading programme. Each set focuses on a particular aspect of phonics: Set 1 – simple short vowel sounds; Set 2 – simple letter strings and double consonants; Set 3 – blends and digraphs; Set 4 – magic 'e'. Key Stages 1 and 2.

Sure Fire Phonics
(Thomas Nelson)
Books containing a variety of exercises to develop phonic skills. Activities include cloze procedure with multi-choice answers, crossword puzzles and picture-word matching. Suitable for Key Stage 2 and above.

Timesaver Phonic Books 1–8
(Precise Educational Publishers Resource Centre, Dainsby House, 18 Market Place, Codnor, Derbyshire DE5 9QA)
Photocopiable sheets in A4 format (40 pages), spirally bound. Activities include matching exercises, finding the odd-one-out and finding missing letters. Suitable for Key Stages 1 and 2.

Tree Worksheets
(Hilda King Educational Services)
Books 1 and 2 contain photocopiable worksheets in A4 format, comb bound (20+ pages). Each worksheet presents a large outline of a tree on which words are printed. Missing letters are inserted by the pupil. The letter omissions focus on a particular phonic element. Key Stages 1 and 2.

The Vowel Sound Book
(Kickstart Publications Ltd)
Photocopiable worksheets (70+ pages) in A4 format, spirally bound. Activities include pencil travel, cut-and-stick matching sounds to pictures, crosswords and cloze procedure. Supplementary activities are included. Suitable for Key Stages 1 and 2.

Young Shorty Story Photocopy Masters
(Ginn and Company)
The Story Workbooks which supported the *Young Shorty Stories* are now available as photocopy masters.

Section 11 – Reading Schemes and Teaching Phonics

All Aboard
(Ginn and Company)
All Aboard is an extensive resource for Key Stages 1 and 2. The core reading books are organised into 14 stages, supported by a wide range of materials and supplementary reading books. At Stages 1, 2 and 3, there are *Pattern and Rhyme* books for developing an awareness of rhyme. Each is accompanied by a workbook. At Stages 1 and 2, the *Pattern and Rhyme* books are available on audio cassettes which include page turn-over signals.

Bangers and Mash
(Longman Group)
This familiar set of phonic readers is intended for pupils in the 5–9 age range. Phonics fit easily and naturally into the stories in the 18 main books. There are two packs of supplementary readers, four workbooks and a teacher's book which contains nine games.

Cambridge Reading
(Cambridge University Press)
Phases 1–3 are Beginning to Read (1); Becoming a Reader (2); and Towards Independence (3). The development of phonological awareness is an integral part of these three phases of the scheme. The link between phonic knowledge and real texts is developed through activities and worksheets in *Teacher's Book 1*, *Listening Pictures* (a flip-over book) and *Sounds Fun!* (a pack of phonic games described elsewhere in this handbook). Phase 1 is intended mainly for pupils in Reception/Primary 1. It builds on their existing knowledge of literacy, especially nursery rhymes. This approach is fully explained in *Teacher's Book 1* which also includes many copy masters to supplement the books.

Flying Boot
(Thomas Nelson)
This resource for Key Stage 1 includes a substantial phonic element with eight consumable workbooks and corresponding copy masters. The workbooks and copy masters cover a range of phonic skills from letter sounds to vowel digraphs and diphthongs. In the *Teacher's Book* there are also three record sheets for phonological awareness.

The introduction concentrates on onset and rime. Both alphabet and sound and rhyme books are available in large and small formats. Accompanying audio cassettes are linked to a CD-ROM.

Fuzzbuzz
(Oxford University Press)
The *Fuzzbuzz* scheme is intended for pupils in Years 6–10 who are experiencing significant difficulty in learning to read.

The presentation of phonics is well suited to this age range. *Letters 1–5* are substantial, consumable phonic workbooks which provide adequate practice in skills ranging from letter sounds to multi-syllabic words. Each workbook is intended to cover the phonic skills needed for the appropriate storybook, once a core sight vocabulary has been established. The work covered by the five books is often sufficient without the use of additional phonic materials. It helps to give pupils confidence to cope with the reading books.

Letterland

(Collins Educational)

Letterland has been developed from Lynn Wendon's original *pictogram* approach. The system involves the fusing of picture cues, or pictograms, into the actual letter shapes in an attempt to provide a mnemonic system of 'built-in' orientation clues. Over the years, this system has been carefully refined and extended to produce a highly sophisticated teaching programme.

Many children enjoy the fun element of this systematic and structured course. *Letterland* is a secret, invisible place, lying somewhere within the written word, and inhabited by fictional characters such as Eddy Elephant, Clever Cat and the Wicked Water Witch. Supporting stories have been developed which explain the behaviour of each letter and the way in which it reacts with other letters.

There are two teaching programmes: *First Steps in Letterland* and *Big Strides in Letterland*. These include work on language; phonic skills; whole-word recognition; reading development and reading for meaning; sentences and early creative writing; and spelling together. Correct letter formation is taught right from the start. Storytelling, singing, drama and role play are an integral part of the learning process.

Certain 'teaching routines' are common throughout with detailed suggestions as to which methods of instruction, routines and materials should be used at each stage.

The extensive range of materials includes teachers' guides; audio and videotapes; upper and lower case letter friezes; song books; picture code cards; computer software; Listen and Write copy masters; finger puppets; Code Sheet copy masters; merit stickers; A-Z peel-off stickers; shuffle card game; Consonant Capers photocopy masters; jigsaw puzzles; and the Letterland Library.

One word of warning should be sounded. Practice has shown that some children can become so involved with the actual characters that they fail to make the necessary association with particular letter sounds, referring simply to 'Annie Apple', 'Vase of Violets' and so forth.

Overall, however, it is felt that the entire system can be highly motivating to children, great fun (for children and teachers alike), and can have a considerable creative and imaginative impact if used fully and correctly.

Longman Book Project

(Longman Group Ltd)

This substantial resource for Key Stages 1 and 2 includes a comprehensive range of phonic materials covering the full range of phonic skills from letter sounds to compound words. A software pack for early phonic skills is included. This progresses from rhyming to C-V-C blending and initial consonant blends. Alphabet cards provide consolidation for letter sounds. Copy masters cover the more advanced phonic elements.

New Reading 360

(Ginn and Company)

The reading books in this scheme are supported by a range of supplementary workbooks designed to develop a range of reading strategies. There are teacher's resource books which include photocopy masters. Some activities for the development of phonic skills are included. However, in situations where an in-depth approach is required, additional phonic resources will be necessary, especially where pupils with special educational needs are concerned.

New Way

(Thomas Nelson)

This scheme is based on a phonic approach with the vocabulary adhering to a phonic hierarchy. There is a phonic workbook for each of the eight colour-coded levels. *Teacher's Guides 1 and 2* are accompanied by a book of photocopiable worksheets and there are also two additional sets of copy masters. They contain games to develop knowledge of letter sounds, blending and a wide range of other skills. The scheme and its supplementary activities may be suitable where a strong emphasis on phonics is required.

Old Reading 360

(Ginn and Company)

There are eight books of copy masters which correspond to the appropriate levels of the reading scheme. Each contains between 18 and 30 worksheets. Although the occasional worksheet in the early stages uses vocabulary from the reading scheme, most of the materials can be used independently and give comprehensive coverage of phonics skills.

Oxford Reading Tree

(Oxford University Press)

The Woodpecker 'branch' is a phonic-based part of the scheme. There are 14 consumable workbooks which cover all the major elements of phonics. The first three books are closely related to the text of the reading books and include consolidation for some of the core sight words. The later workbooks can be used independently of the scheme. Letter sounds are covered in upper and lower case forms and are revised throughout the early books. There is adequate material for C-V-C blending practice, and initial and final consonant blends are well covered.

The presentation is intended for pupils in Years 1 and 2. A significant amount of teacher guidance is required. For most pupils, there are sufficient materials for them to acquire a foundation of phonic skills without the use of additional items.

Wellington Square

(Thomas Nelson)

This scheme has been specifically designed for children who are experiencing difficulty with their reading. It is a library of resources comprising a range of materials arranged in five levels. In addition to a set of Language Master cards which cover the vocabulary for Level 1, there are software packages published by Wellysoft and SEMERC.

A range of helpful information can be found in the five *Teacher's Resource Packs*. The sections on phonics include work on blending short vowel sounds and consonant digraphs. There is also a Phonic Index which lists items in the scheme alphabetically, giving their reading levels and reference numbers for appropriate worksheets.

Section 12 – Index of Phonic Resources

Visual Discrimination

New Pencil Play 1 (Collins)

Let's Look (LDA)
Sequential Thinking Cards 1–5 (LDA)

Visual Recall Flash Cards (LDA)

Oxford Junior Workbooks (Oxford University Press)
Book 4, Page 36
Book 5, Pages 28, 42
Book 6, Pages 10, 24, 28

Book 7, Page 16
Book 8, Pages 20, 42

Coloured Cube Designs (Taskmaster)

Easigrip Pegboard and Pegs (Taskmaster)
Sequencing Bead Patterns (Taskmaster)
Sequencing Beads (Taskmaster)

Soft Touch Letters (Taskmaster)
Tac Tiles (Taskmaster)
Visual Variants (Taskmaster)
What's Missing? (Taskmaster)

Auditory discrimination

Look Hear (LDA)
Photo Sound Lotto (LDA)
Sound Stories (LDA)
Stile Phonics Book 1, Pages 3, 8, 14 (all from LDA)
　　　　　　　Book 2, Pages 9, 10
　　　　　　　Book 3, Pages 7–12
　　　　　　　Book 4, Pages 5–9, 11–13, 16
　　　　　　　Book 5, Pages 1–16
　　　　　　　Book 6, Pages 1–14
　　　　　　　Book 7, Pages 1–4, 6, 7, 10, 12
　　　　　　　Book 8, Pages 2, 4, 5, 7, 9, 10, 12
　　　　　　　Book 9, Pages 9, 16
　　　　　　　Book 11, Page 13
　　　　　　　Book 12, Pages 9, 10, 13

Listen! (Learning Materials Ltd.)
Listen and Colour 1, 2 (Learning Materials Ltd.)
Listen, Colour and Write (Learning Materials Ltd.)
Pictures in Sound A, B, C (Learning Materials Ltd.)
Reason and Write 1–5 (Learning Materials Ltd.)
Sentence Making Kit (Learning Materials Ltd.)
Snowman Kit 1, 2, 3 (Learning Materials Ltd.)
Sound Discrimination (Learning Materials Ltd.)
Sound Lotto 1, 2, 3 (Learning Materials Ltd.)

Oxford Junior Workbook 7, Page 15 (OUP)

SRA Schoolhouse, Word Skills 1, Violet Cards 1–25

Familiar Sounds (Taskmaster)
Listening Discrimination Balls (Taskmaster)
Listening Lotto-ry (Taskmaster)

Phonological Awareness
Rhyming

Flying Boot – Big Sound and Rhyme Book (The)
         – My Alphabet Fold-a-Book
         – Patterns and Rhyme
         – Phonic Book 2
         – Phonic Rhyme Time
         – Sound and Rhyme Tapes
Phonic Worksheets (Prim-Ed)
Rhyme and Analogy – Story Rhyme Photocopy Masters
         – Story Rhyme Reading Books
         – Story Rhyme Tapes

Initial Letter Sounds

Active Phonics, Workbooks 1, 2 and 3
Alpha to Omega, Stage 1, Page 4
Language 1 – Alphabet Cards
Rhyme and Analogy – Alphabet Frieze
Rhyme and Analogy – Alphabet Photocopy Masters
The Big Book of Early Phonics
Cloze and Phonic Activities Books 1–4
Duncan Dragon, Sound Book 1, Pages 2–8, 14, 15 (O/P)
Finger Phonics, Books 1–6
Flying Boot – Phonic Book 1
Fuzzbuzz, Letters Book 1, Pages 4, 6, 7, 8, 10, 11, 13, 22, 23,
25–36, 42–56
Ginn 360, Duplicating Masters, Level 2b
                          Level 3 Sheet 1

Ginn Phonic Workbook 2, Pages 3–6, 9, 13, 14–16
Language 1 Books
Letter Sound Book (The)
Language 1 Copymasters C19, C20, C22, C33, C34, C35
Language 1 Alphabet Collage Sheets
New Phonic Blending 1, 2
Oxford Junior Workbook Book 4, Pages 17, 23, 33, 37, 39, 41,
43–45
                  Book 5, Pages 5, 7, 22, 25, 39, 40
                  Book 6, Page 44
                  Book 6, Pages 25, 33
Phonic Bank Card 2
Phonic Links 1 and 2
The Phonics Book (Stanley Thornes)
Phonics Book 1
The Phonics Handbook
Phonics - Resource Bank and Teachers' Guide Sheets A6, A7

Reading Quest 2, Pages 3–16 (O/P)
The Second Letter Sound Book
Young Shorty Activity Book 1, Pages 1, 6, 7, 8, 11, 12, 18, 26, 27, 29
Young Shorty Activity Book 2, Pages 2, 3, 10, 11
Sound Practice Book 2, Pages 3–10, 30
Soundstart Phonics Workshop 1
Sounds Alive, Reinforcement Sheets
SRA Schoolhouse Violet, Cards 6–20
       Tan, Cards 1–26
       Lime, Cards 23–26
Stile Early Phonics
Stile Phonic Practice Cards 1–4, 12, 13, 17, 26
Stile Phonics, Book 1, Pages 1–16
       Book 2, Pages 1–16
Sure-fire Phonics, Book 2, Pages 2, 4, 5, 7–24
Sure-fire Phonics, Book 1, Pages 9–24, 26–29
Rhyme and Analogy – Tabletop Alphabet Pack
Timesavers, Phonic Book 1
Oxford Reading Tree – Woodpecker, Workbook A, Pages 3–5, 8–10, 12–14
Woodpecker, Workbook B, Pages 1–16
Woodpecker, Workbook C, Pages 2, 4, 6, 8, 9, 11, 12, 14, 15
Woodpecker, Workbook D, Pages 2, 4, 5, 7, 8
Woodpecker, Workbook E, Pages 4, 7
Woodpecker, Workbook 1, Pages 2, 15, 16
Woodpecker, Workbook 2, Pages 12–16

Final Letter Sounds

Active Phonics, Workbooks 1 and 2
Duncan Dragon, Sound Book 1, Pages 9–13, Page 16 (O/P)
Flying Boot – Phonic Book 1
Fuzzbuzz, Letters Book 1, Pages 39, 40, 58
Fuzzbuzz, Letters Book 2, Pages 13, 14
*Ginn 360, Duplicating Masters, Level 3, Sheets 2–11
Ginn Phonic Workbook 1, Page 18
Ginn Phonic Workbook 2, Pages 1, 19
Key Phonics, Book 1
The Letter Sound Book
Phonic Links 2
The Phonics Handbook (Stanley Thornes)
Reading Quest 2, Pages 17–24 (O/P)
The Second Letter Sound Book
Young Shorty Activity Book 1, Pages 11, 12
SRA Schoolhouse, Violet, Cards 21–24
       Lime, Cards 1–16
Sound Practice, Book 2, Pages 15–26
Woodpecker, Workbook C, Pages 10, 13, 16
Woodpecker, Workbook D, Pages 3, 6, 9, 12, 14, 15
Woodpecker, Workbook E, Pages 2, 3, 5, 6, 8, 11, 12, 15, 16

* Note that all *Reading 360* materials referred to are part of the old version.

Woodpecker, Workbook 1, Page 3
Woodpecker, Workbook 2, Pages 2–11, 13–16
Woodpecker, Workbook 3, Pages 4, 6, 8

'qu'   Active Phonics, Workbook 2
The bdpq Reading and Writing Book
Cloze and Phonic Activities, Book 6, Pages 9–11
Finger Phonics, Book 7
Ginn 360, Duplicating Masters, Level 7, Sheet 2
Key Phonics, Book 3, Page 22
Language 1, Copymaster C20
The Letter Sound Book
Phonic Bank, Card 20
Phonic Blending, Book 3, Lesson 7
Phonics - Bank Teachers' Guide Sheets P4, P5
The Phonics Handbook (Stanley Thornes)
Reading Quest 3, Pages 32, 33 (O/P)
The Second Letter Sound Book

SRA Schoolhouse, Rose, Card 6
Sure-fire Phonics, Book 4, Page 9

Short 'a'   Breaking the Code, Book 1
Crosswords 2
Duncan Dragon, Sound Book 1, Pages 18–23 (O/P)
The First Phonic Blending Book
Fuzzbuzz, Letters Book 1, Pages 4, 5
Ginn 360, Duplicating Masters, Level 4, Sheets 1, 2, 4
Language 1, Copymaster C55
Language 1, Teacher's Resource Book, Pages 35, 116, 163
Learning Phonics 2, Cassette 1
Phonic Bank, Cards 3, 4
Phonics – Resource Bank and Teachers' Guide Sheet A5
Flying Boot – Phonic Book 2
The Phonics Book (Stanley Thornes)
The Phonics Handbook
Young Shorty Activity Book 1, Pages 6, 7, 8, 11, 12
Soundstart Phonics Workshop 1
Sounds Easy, Level 0, Book 1
Stile Phonics, Book 1, Pages 1–3
Supersonic, Reading Book 'Ragbag'
Sure-fire Phonics, Book 1, Page 2
SRA Schoolhouse, Orange, Card 1
Sound Practice, Book 2, Page 11
Sound Practice, Book 3, Pages 3, 4, 17, 18
Sound Sense, Book 1, Pages 2, 3 (O/P)
Timesavers, Phonic Book 3
The Vowel Sound Book

Short 'e'

Breaking the Code, Book 1
Crosswords 2
Duncan Dragon, Sound Book 2, Page 4
The First Phonic Blending Book
Flying Boot - Phonic Book 2
Fuzzbuzz, Letters Book 1, Page 7, 8
Ginn 360, Duplicating Masters, Level 4, Sheet 5
Learning Phonics 2, Cassette 1
Language 1, Copymaster C53
Phonic Bank Cards 5 and 6
The Phonics Book (Stanley Thornes)
Phonics – Resource Bank and Teachers' Guide Sheet A5
The Phonics Handbook
Young Shorty Activity Book 1, Pages 26–29
Sound Practice, Book 2, Page 11
Sound Practice, Book 3, Pages 5, 6, 19, 20
Sound Sense, Book 1, Pages 6, 7 (O/P)
Soundstart Phonics, Workshop 1
Sounds Easy, Level 0, Book 4
Sure-fire Phonics, Book 1, Page 3
SRA Schoolhouse, Orange, Card 2
Stile Phonics, Book 1, Pages 4, 5
Supersonic Reading Book 'Beth's Bed'
Timesavers, Phonic Book 3
The Vowel Sound Book

Short 'i'

Breaking the Code, Book 1
Crosswords 2
Duncan Dragon, Sound Book 2, Pages 2, 3, 11 (O/P)
The First Phonic Blending Book
Flying Boot – Phonic Book 2
Fuzzbuzz, Letters Book 1, Pages 10, 12
Ginn 360, Duplicating Masters, Level 3, Sheets 12–19
Learning Phonics 2, Cassette 1
Phonic Bank, Cards 7, 8
The Phonics Book (Stanley Thornes)
Phonics – Resource Bank and Teachers' Guide Sheet A5
The Phonics Handbook
Young Shorty Activity Book 1, Pages 18, 21
Sound Practice, Book 2, Page 11
Sound Practice, Book 3, Pages 7, 8, 21, 22
Sound Sense, Book 1, Pages 4, 5
Soundstart Phonics Workshop 1
Sounds Easy, Level 0, Book 3
SRA Schoolhouse, Orange, Card 3
Stile Phonics, Book 1, Pages 6–8
Supersonic, Reading Book 'Is Jim In?'
Sure-fire Phonics, Book 1, Page 4
Timesavers, Phonic Book 3
The Vowel Sound Book

Short 'o'

Breaking the Code, Book 1
Crosswords 2
Duncan Dragon, Sound Book 2, Page 5
The First Phonic Blending Book
Flying Boot – Phonic Book 2
Fuzzbuzz, Letters Book 1, Pages 22, 24
Ginn 360, Duplicating Masters, Level 4, Sheet 7
                                           Level 5, Sheet 4

Learning Phonics 2, Cassette 1
Language 1, Copymaster C52
Phonic Bank, Cards 9, 10
Phonics – Resource Bank and Teachers' Guide Sheet A5
The Phonics Book (Stanley Thornes)
The Phonics Handbook
Young Shorty Activity Book 1, Pages 18, 21
Sound Practice, Book 2, Page 11
Sound Practice, Book 3, Pages 9, 10, 23, 24
Sound Sense, Book 1, Pages 8, 9 (O/P)
Soundstart Phonics Workshop 1
Sounds Easy, Level 0, Book 2
SRA Schoolhouse, Orange, Card 4
Stile Phonics, Book 1, Page 9
Supersonic, Reading Book 'Hippo Pot' and 'Hippo Tot'
Sure-fire Phonics, Book 1, Page 5
Timesavers, Phonic Book 3
The Vowel Sound Book

Short 'u'

Breaking the Code, Book 1
Crosswords 2
The First Phonic Blending Book
Flying Boot – Phonic Book 2
Fuzzbuzz, Letters Book 1, Pages 13, 15
Ginn 360, Duplicating Masters, Level 4, Sheet 3
Ginn 360, Duplicating Masters, Level 5, Sheet 3
Learning Phonics 2, Cassette 1
Language 1, Copymaster C54
Phonics – Resource Bank and Teachers' Guide Sheet A5
The Phonics Book (Stanley Thornes)
The Phonics Handbook
Young Shorty Activity Book 2, Pages 2, 3, 5
Sound Practice, Book 2, Page 12
Sound Practice, Book 3, Pages 11, 12, 25, 26
Sound Sense, Book 1, Pages 10, 11 (O/P)
Soundstart Phonics Workshop 1
Sounds Easy, Level 0, Book 5
SRA Schoolhouse, Orange, Card 5
Stile Phonics, Book 1, Pages 7, 10
Supersonic Reading Book 'Hup Pups'
Sure-fire Phonics, Book 1, Page 6
Timesavers, Phonic Book 3
The Vowel Sound Book

Short Vowel Revision	Active Phonics, Workbooks 2 and 3
	Alpha to Omega, Stage 1, Page 13
	Breaking the Code, Book 1
	Duncan Dragon, Sound Book 2, Page 6 (O/P)
	Fuzzbuzz, Letters Book 2, Page 3
	Ginn 360, Duplicating Masters, Level 4, Sheets 6, 8
	Level 5, Sheet 1
	Language 1, Copymasters C36, C50
	Phonic Bank, Cards 11, 12
	Phonic Bank, PCM 1
	Phonic Blending, Book 1, Lessons 1–16
	Phonic Ladders
	Phonics (Easylearn) Book 2
	Phonics – Resource Bank and Teachers' Guide Sheets A5, A7
	Reading Quest, 2, Pages 27, 31 (O/P)
	Young Shorty Activity Book 2, Pages 22, 23, 25, 28, 31
	Young Shorty Activity Book 1, Page 1
	Sound Practice, Book 3, Pages 13–16, 30, 3l
	Sound Sense, Book 1, Pages 12–16, 18, 23 (O/P)
	SRA Schoolhouse, Orange, Cards 6, 11, 13, 21
	Stile Phonics Book 1, Pages 11–13, 15, 16
	Book 2, Pages 1–8, 11–16
	Book 4, Pages 1–7
	Stile Phonic Practice Cards 1–6
	Supersonic, Reading Book 'Bot's Bits'
	Sure-fire Phonics, Book 1, Page 7
	Sure-fire Phonics, Book 3, Pages 2, 4, 5, 9–17
	Timesavers, Phonic Book 3
	The Vowel Sound Book
	Woodpecker, Workbook 3, Pages 2, 3, 5, 7, 9, 10, 11–14
'b-d-p' confusion	The bdpq Reading and Writing Book
	Helper Books 3, 4, 5
	Language 1, Copymaster C25
	Phonic Blending Book 1, Lessons 1, 2, 13
	Phonics (Easylearn) Book 3
	Sound Practice, Book 2, Page 29
	Specific Learning Difficulties Phonic Skills Book 1
	Timesaver, Phonic Book 8
	Timesaver b d p Book
Final Double Consonants 'ff'	Active Phonics, Workbook 4
	Alpha to Omega, Stage 1, Page 62
	Ginn 360, Duplicating Masters, Level 9, Sheets 2, 3
	Ginn Phonic Workbook 2, Page 10
	The Phonics Book (Stanley Thornes)
	Specific Learning Difficulties Spelling Rules Book 1
	Supersonic Reading Books, Set 2
	Woodpecker, Workbook E, Page 14
	Woodpecker, Workbook 4, Page 3
	Woodpecker, Workbook 5, Page 2

'll'   Active Phonics, Workbook 4
         Alpha to Omega, Stage 1, Pages 60, 63
         Crosswords 1–3
         Ginn Phonic Workbook 2, Page 10
         Key Phonics, Book 3, Pages 31, 33
         Learning Phonics 1, Cassette 1
         Language 1, Copymasters C48, C51
         Phonic Ladders
         The Phonics Book (Stanley Thornes)
         Reading Quest 4, Pages 40, 41 (O/P)
         Sound Practice, Book 4, Page 26
         Soundstart, Phonic Workshop 2
         SpLD Spelling Rules Book 1
         Stile Phonics, Book 8, Page 1
         Supersonics Reading Books, Set 2
         Timesavers, Phonic Book 1
         Tree Worksheets 1–3
         Woodpecker, Workbook 4, Pages 2, 16
         Woodpecker, Workbook 5, Page 1

'ss'   Active Phonics, Workbook 4
         Alpha to Omega, Stage 1, Pages 61, 70
         Breaking the Code, Book 2
         Ginn Phonic Workbook 2, Page 10
         Language 1, Copymaster C51
         The Phonics Book (Stanley Thornes)
         Specific Learning Difficulties Spelling Rules Book 1
         Supersonics, Reading Books, Set 2
         Timesavers, Phonic Book 1
         Woodpecker, Workbook 4, Page 3
         Woodpecker, Workbook 5, Page 2

'ck'   Active Phonics, Workbook 4
         Breaking the Code, Book 2
         Cloze and Phonic Activities, Book 8, Pages 4–6
         Crosswords 2
         Flying Boot – Phonic Book 2
         Fuzzbuzz, Letters Book 2, Pages 7, 9
         Ginn 360, Duplicating Masters, Level 5, Sheet 20
         Key Phonics, Blending Book 2, Lesson 1
         Learning Phonics 2, Cassette 6
         Language 1, Copymasters C48, C51
         Phonics – Resource Bank and Teachers' Guide Sheets E10, E11
         The Phonics Book (Stanley Thornes)
         The Phonics Handbook
         Read Write and Spell, Stage 2, Pages 34, 35
         Reading Quest 3, Pages 14, 15 (O/P)
         SRA Schoolhouse, Rose, Card 8
         Soundstart Phonic, Workshop 2
         Specific Learning Difficulties Spelling Rules Book 1
         Supersonics Reading Books Set 2

Sure-fire Phonics, Book 4, Page 14
Timesavers, Phonic Book 1

Final Consonant Blends   **'mp'**   Active Phonics, Workbook 6
Cloze and Phonic Activities, Book 8, Pages 14–16
Learning Phonics 2, Cassette 6
Language 1, Copymaster C51
Soundstart Phonic Workshop 2

     'nd'   Active Phonics, Workbook 6
Cloze and Phonic Activities, Book 8, Pages 17–19
Learning Phonics 2, Cassette 6
Soundstart Phonic Workshop 2

     'ng'   Active Phonics, Workbook 4
Finger Phonics, Book 5
Learning Phonics 1, Cassette 2
Phonic Links, Book 3, Worksheets 7, 8
Soundstart Phonics Workshop 2

     'nk'   Active Phonics, Workbook 4
Crosswords 2
Cloze and Phonic Activities, Book 8, Pages 20–22
Learning Phonics 2, Cassette 6
Language 1, Copymaster C51
Reading Quest 3, Pages 6, 7 (O/P)
Soundstart Phonics Workshop 2
SRA Schoolhouse, Rose, Card 8
Supersonics Reading Books, Set 2
Sure-fire Phonics, Book 4, Page 14

     'nt'   Active Phonics, Workbook 6
Cloze and Phonic Activities, Book 8, Pages 23–25
Ginn 360, Duplicating Masters, Level 6, Sheets 11, 12
Key Phonics, Book 2, Pages 26, 29
The Phonics Book (Stanley Thornes)
Soundstart Phonic Workshop 2
SRA Schoolhouse, Rose, Card 7
Supersonics, Reading Books, Set 2
Sure-fire Phonics, Book 4, Page 11
Woodpecker, Workbook E, Page 9

     'pt'   Ginn 360, Duplicating Masters, Level 8, Sheet 9
The Phonics Book (Stanley Thornes)

     'sk'   Cloze and Phonic Activities, Book 8, Pages 26–28
SRA Schoolhouse, Rose, Card 8
Sound Practice, Book 5, Page 26

     'st'   Sound and Phonic Activities, Book 8, Pages 30–32
Soundstart Phonic Workshop 2

Final Consonant **Blend Revision**		Active Phonics, Workbooks 4 and 6
		Alpha to Omega, Stage 1, Pages 31–33
		Flying Boot – Phonic Book 4
		Key Phonics, Book 2, Page 29
		Language 1, Copymaster C51
		Phonic Blending, Book 1, Lessons 3–15
		Phonic Ladders
		SRA Schoolhouse, Rose, Cards 9, 10
		Stile Phonics, Book 3, Pages 5, 6, 13–16
		Book 4, Pages 4, 10, 14, 15
		Book 5, Pages 3, 6, 13
		Book 6, Pages 1–3, 8, 10, 16
		Book 7, Pages 3, 5, 8, 9, 12, 13
		Book 8, Pages 5, 6, 8, 13, 15, 16
		Stile Phonic, Practice Cards 3–5, 11, 12, 14
		Supersonics, Reading Books, Sets 2 and 3
Consonant **Digraphs**	'ch'	Active Phonics, Workbook 3
		Alpha to Omega, Stage 1, Pages 19–21
		Breaking the Code, Book 2
		The Consonant Digraph Book
		Crossword 15
		Finger Phonics, Book 6
		Flying Boot – Phonic Book 3
		Fuzzbuzz, Letters Book 2, Pages 4, 5
		Ginn 360, Duplicating Sheets, Level 4, Sheets 17, 18
		Level 5, Sheet 2
		Level 9, Sheets 4, 5
		Key Phonics, Book 3, Pages 2, 5
		Book 4, Page 7
		Learning Phonics 1, Cassette 4
		Language 1, Copymasters C22, C38
		New Phonic Blending 3
		Phonic Bank, Card 13
		Phonic Blending, Book 2, Lesson 5
		Phonic Ladders
		Phonic Links, Book 3, Worksheet 15
		The Phonics Book (Stanley Thornes)
		The Phonics Handbook
		Phonics – Resource Bank and Teachers' Guide, Sheets E2, E3
		Read Write and Spell, Stage 2, Page 12
		Reading Quest 3, Pages 26, 27 (O/P)
		Young Shorty, Book 1, Pages 12, 13, 14
		Sound Practice, Book 4, Pages 27, 28
		Sound Sense, Book 5, Pages 31–35 (O/P)
		Soundstart Phonic Workshop 2
		Specific Learning Difficulties Phonic Skills, Book 1
		Specific Learning Difficulties Spelling Rules, Book 1
		SRA Schoolhouse, Rose, Card 13
		Stile Phonics, Book 3, Pages 7, 10–12

Book 4, Pages 2, 9
Book 5, Page 1
Book 7, Page 2
Supersonics, Reading Books, Set 2
Sure-fire Phonics, Book 4, Page 3
Timesavers, Phonic Book 4
Tree Worksheet 15
Woodpecker, Workbook 4, Page 11

'ch' (chemist)   Ginn 360, Duplicating Masters, Level 9
                                       Level 6
Phonics – Resource Bank and Teachers' Guide Sheets E5, E6
Reading Quest 5, Page 23 (O/P)

Specific Learning Difficulties Phonic Skills, Book 1
Sounds and Words, Book 6, Page 19
Specific Learning Difficulties Phonic Skills, Book 1
Stile Phonics, Book 12, Page 15

'sh'   Active Phonics, Workbook 3
Alpha to Omega, Stage 1, Pages 19–21, 23–25
Breaking the Code, Book 2
The Consonant Digraph Book
Crosswords 13
Finger Phonics, Book 6
Flying Boot – Phonic Book 3
Fuzzbuzz, Letters Book 2, Pages 10, 11
Ginn 360, Duplicating Masters, Level 4, Sheets 16, 18
                                 Level 5, Sheet 14
                                 Level 9, Sheet 4

Key Phonics, Book 3, Pages 1, 5
Learning Phonics 1, Cassette 4
Language 1, Copymasters C22, C37
New Phonic Blending, 3
Phonic Bank, Card 15
Phonic Blending, Book 1, Lesson 17
Phonic Ladders
The Phonics Book (Stanley Thornes)
The Phonics Handbook
Phonics – Resource Bank and Teachers' Guide Sheets E1, E3
Read Write and Spell, Stage 2, Page 8
Reading Quest 3, Pages 24, 25 (O/P)
Young Shorty Activity Book 1, Pages 10, 11, 14, 18
Sound Practice, Book 4, Pages 29–30
Sound Sense, Book 5, Pages 2, 3, 5 (O/P)
Soundstart Phonics Workshop 2
Specific Learning Difficulties Phonic Skills Book 1
SRA Schoolhouse, Rose, Card 14
Stile Phonics, Book 3, Pages 1, 4, 5, 7, 10–12, 16
                     Book 4, Pages 2, 9
                     Book 5, Page 1
                     Book 7, Page 2

Sure-fire Phonics, Book 4, Page 2
Timesavers, Phonic Book 4
Tree Worksheet 12
Woodpecker, Workbook 4, Pages 11, 13

'th'   Active Phonics, Workbook 3
Alpha to Omega, Stage 1, Pages 24, 25
Breaking the Code, Book 2
The Consonant Digraph Book
Crosswords 2
Duncan Dragon Sound, Book 2, Page 19 (O/P)
Finger Phonics, Book 6
Flying Boot – Phonic Book 3
Fuzzbuzz, Letters Book 2, Pages 7, 8
Ginn 360, Duplicating Masters, Level 5, Sheets 17, 18
Key Phonics, Book 3, Pages 3, 5
Learning Phonics 2, Cassette 5
Language 1, Copymaster C22, C39
New Phonic Blending 3
Phonic Bank, Card 14
Phonic Blending, Book 2, Lesson 3
The Phonics Book (Stanley Thornes)
Phonics – Resource Bank and Teachers' Guide Sheet E8
The Phonics Handbook
Read Write and Spell, Stage 2, Page 16
Reading Quest 3, Pages 30, 31 (O/P)
Young Shorty Activity Book 1, Pages 16, 17, 18
Sound Practice, Book 5, Page 4
Sound Sense, Book 5, Pages 16,17 (O/P)
Soundstart Phonics Workshop 2
Specific Learning Difficulties Phonic Skills Book 1
SRA Schoolhouse, Rose, Card 15
Stile Phonics, Book 3, Pages 4, 7, 12, 16,
                Book 4, Page 2
                Book 5, Page 12
Sure-fire Phonics, Book 4, Pages 5, 6
The Consonant Digraph Book
Woodpecker, Workbook 4, Pages 11, 13, 15

'wh'   Alpha to Omega, Stage 1, Pages 24, 25
The Consonant Digraph Book
Crosswords 2
Flying Boot – Phonic Book 3
Ginn 360, Duplicating Masters, Level 5, Sheet 15
Key Phonics, Book 3, Pages 4, 5
Learning Phonics 2, Cassette 5
Phonic Bank, Card 41
Phonics – Resource Bank and Teachers' Guide Sheet E9
Reading Quest 3, Pages 28, 29 (O/P)
SpLD Phonic Skills Book 1

Read Write and Spell, Stage 2, Page 60
Sound Sense, Book 6, Page 2 (O/P)
Soundstart Phonics Workshop 2
Specific Learning Difficulties Phonic Skills Book 1
SRA Schoolhouse, Rose, Card 15
Stile Phonics, Book 3, Pages 12, 16
                 Book 7, Page 2
Sure-fire Phonics, Book 4, Page 7
Woodpecker, Workbook 4, Page 12

'ph'   The Consonant Digraph Book
Ginn 360, Duplicating Masters, Level 9, Sheets 22, 23
Key Phonics, Book 4, Page 1
Phonic Bank, Card 41
Phonic Workshop, Card 47
Phonics – Resource Bank and Teachers' Guide Sheets Q7, Q8
Read Write and Spell, Stage 4, Page 42
Reading Quest 5, Page 22 (O/P)
Sound Sense, Book 8, Pages 39, 40 (O/P)
Sounds and Words, Book 5, Page 4
Specific Learning Difficulties Phonic Skills Book 1

Consonant Digraph
Revision   The Consonant Digraph Book
Language 1, Copymaster C40
Phonic Bank PCM 2
Phonics, Book 6
Reading Quest 3, Pages 34, 35 (O/P)
Specific Learning Difficulties Phonic Skills Book 1
Stile Phonic Practice Cards, 22, 25, 26, 29, 30
SRA Schoolhouse, Rose, Cards 17–19, 21, 22
Supersonics, Reading Books, Set 3

Long Consonant
Digraphs   **'shr'**   The Consonant Digraph Book
Phonic Blending, Book 3, Lesson 7
Phonics – Resource Bank and Teachers' Guide Sheet F5
Specific Learning Difficulties Phonic Skills Book 1
Woodpecker, Workbook 8, Pages 5, 6

'tch'   The Consonant Digraph Book
Fuzzbuzz, Letters Book 2, Page 43
Ginn 360, Duplicating Masters, Level 6, Sheet 20
                                     Level 9, Sheet 5
Key Phonics, Book 4, Page 5
Language 1, Copymaster C51
Phonic Blending, Book 3, Lessons 5, 12
Phonic Ladders
Phonic Links, Book 3, Worksheets 16
Phonics – Resource Bank and Teachers' Guide Sheet E4
Read Write and Spell, Stage 3, Page 40
Sound Sense, Book 5, Pages 32, 33 (O/P)

Specific Learning Difficulties Phonic Skills Book 1
Specific Learning Difficulties Spelling Rules Book 1
Stile Phonics, Book 7, Pages 2–4
           Book 8, Page 11
           Book 12, Pages 5, 6
Sure-fire Phonics, Book 4, Page 4
Woodpecker, Workbook 4, Page 15

'thr'   Ginn 360, Duplicating Masters, Level 7, Sheet 24
Phonic Blending, Book 3, Lesson 11
Phonics – Resource Bank and Teachers' Guide, Sheet F5
Specific Learning Difficulties, Phonic Skills, Book 1
Woodpecker, Workbook 8, Pages 3, 4

Magic 'e' (a)   Active Phonics, Workbook 5
Alpha to Omega, Stage 1, Page 82
Breaking the Code, Book 3
Crosswords 23
Duncan Dragon, Sound Book 2, Page 20 (O/P)
Fuzzbuzz, Letters Book 5, Pages 3–7
Ginn 360, Duplicating Masters, Level 4, Sheet 13–15
           Level 5, Sheet 19
Key Phonics, Book 3, Page 17
Language 1, Teacher's Resource Book, Pages 163, 199
Learning Phonics, Cassette 6, Sides 1, 2
The Magic 'e' Book
New Phonic Blending 3
Phonic Bank, Card 29
Phonic Ladders
The Phonics Book (Stanley Thornes)
Phonics – Resource Bank and Teachers' Guide, Sheet B2
Read Write and Spell, Stage 2, Pages 38, 39
Reading Quest 4, Pages 8, 9 (O/P)
Young Shorty Activity Book 2, Page 7
Sound Sense, Book 3, Pages 2–4 (O/P)
Soundstart Phonic Workshop 2
Specific Learning Difficulties Phonic Skill 1
Supersonics, Reading Book 'Jake the Snake'
Sure-fire Phonics Book 4, Page 19
Timesaver, Phonic Book 8
Tree Worksheets 20, 21
Woodpecker, Workbook 1, Page 5

Magic 'e' (i)   Active Phonics, Workbook 5
Breaking the Code, Book 3
Crosswords 22, 24
Duncan Dragon, Sound Book 2, Page 21 (O/P)
Fuzzbuzz, Letters Book 5, Pages 8–12
Ginn 360, Duplicating Masters, Level 4, Sheets 9–11
           Level 5, Sheet 19
Key Phonic, Book 3, Page 19

Learning Phonics, Cassette 6, Sides 1, 2
The Magic 'e' Book
New Phonic Blending 3
Phonic Bank, Card 30
Phonic Ladders
Phonics – Resource Bank and Teachers' Guide Sheets C1, C2
The Phonics Book (Stanley Thornes)
Read Write and Spell, Stage 2, Pages 40, 41
Reading Quest 4, Pages 10, 11 (O/P)
Young Shorty Activity Book 2, Page 9
Sound Sense, Book 3, Pages 9, 10 (O/P)
Soundstart, Phonic Workshop 2
Sounds and Words, Book 2, Pages 17, 18
Specific Learning Difficulties Phonic Skills Book 1
Supersonics, Reading Book 'Mike's Bike'
Sure-fire Phonics, Book 4, Page 20
Timesaver, Phonic Book 8
Tree Worksheets 22, 24
Woodpecker, Workbook 1, Page 12

Magic 'e' (o)

Active Phonics, Workbook 5
Breaking the Code, Book 3
Fuzzbuzz, Letters Book 5, Pages 13–17
Ginn 360, Duplicating Masters, Level 5, Sheet 4
Key Phonics, Book 3, Page 18
The Magic 'e' Book
New Phonic Blending 3
Phonic Bank, Card 31
Phonic Ladders
Phonics – Resource Bank and Teachers' Guide Sheets C3, C5
The Phonics Book (Stanley Thornes)
Read Write and Spell, Stage 2, Pages 42, 43
Reading Quest 4, Pages 12, 13 (O/P)
Young Shorty Activity Book 2, Page 8
Sound Sense, Book 3, Pages 16, 17 (O/P)
Soundstart Phonic Workshop 2
Specific Learning Difficulties Phonic Skills Book 1
Supersonics, Reading Book 'Skittles and Skullbones'
Sure-fire Phonics, Book 4, Page 21
Timesaver, Phonic Book 8

Magic 'e' (u)

Active Phonics, Workbook 5
Breaking the Code, Book 3
Fuzzbuzz, Letters Book 5, Pages 18–22
Ginn 360, Duplicating Masters, Level 5, Sheet 3
Key Phonics, Book 3, Page 20
The Magic 'e' Book
New Phonic Blending 3
Phonic Bank, Card 31
The Phonics Book (Stanley Thornes)
Phonics – Resource Bank and Teachers' Guide Sheets C6, C7

Reading Quest 4, Pages 14, 15 (O/P)
Soundstart Phonic Workshop 2
Sure-fire Phonics, Book 4, Page 22
Timesaver, Phonic Book 8
Woodpecker, Workbook 7, Page 5

Magic 'e' Revision

Duncan Dragon, Sound Book 2, Page 22 (O/P)
Flying Boot – Phonic Books, 3 and 4
Ginn Phonic Workbook 5, Pages 1, 2
Key Phonics, Book 3, Page 21
        Book 4, Page 25
The Magic 'e' Book
Phonic Bank PCM 8
Phonic Blending, Book 2, Lessons 13, 14
Phonics Book 7
Sound Practice, Book 5, Pages 28, 31
Specific Learning Difficulties Phonic Skills Book 1
SRA Schoolhouse, Orange, Cards 14, 15, 22
Stile Phonics, Book 6, Pages 14, 15
        Book 9, Pages 1–7
        Book 10, Pages 14,16
Stile Phonic Practice Cards 18–20
Supersonics, Reading Book 'Whoops!'
Timesaver, Phonic Book 8
Woodpecker, Workbook 7, Pages 1, 4, 6, 7, 9, 11–14, 16

Initial Consonant Blends with 'i' General

Active Phonics, Workbook 4
Cloze and Phonic Activities, Book 5
Fuzzbuzz, Letters Book 2, Page 21
Language 1, Copymasters C40–C43
Phonic Blending, Book 2, Lesson 11
The Phonics Book (Stanley Thornes)
Young Shorty Activity Book 1, Page 26
Sound Practice, Book 4, Page 10, 20–23
SRA Schoolhouse, Rose, Card 2
Woodpecker, Workbook 5, Pages 5, 6

Individual Initial Consonant Blends

'bl'
Crosswords 2
Ginn 360, Duplicating Masters, Level 6, Sheet 10
Learning Phonics 2, Cassette 3
Phonic Links, Book 3, Worksheets 11, 18
Read Write and Spell, Stage 2, Pages 19, 20
Sound Practice, Book 4, Page 3
Sound Sense, Book 6, Pages 6, 7 (O/P)
Soundstart Phonic Workshop 2

'cl'
Crosswords 2
Ginn 360, Duplicating Masters, Level 5, Sheets 12, 14
Learning Phonics 2, Cassette 3
Phonic Links, Book 3, Worksheets 11, 14
Read Write and Spell, Stage 2, Pages 19, 20

Sound Practice, Book 4, Page 4
Sound Sense, Book 6, Pages 18, 19 (O/P)
Soundstart Phonic Workshop 2
Woodpecker, Workbook 4, Page 7

'fl' Phonic Links, Book 3, Worksheets 6, 18
Sound Practice, Book 4, Page 5
Sound Sense, Book 6, Pages 17, 18 (O/P)
Woodpecker, Workbook 4, Page 7

'gl' Ginn 360, Duplicating Masters, Level 5, Sheet 16
Phonic Links, Book 3, Worksheet 38
Sound Practice, Book 4, Page 4
Sure-fire Phonics, Book 5, Page 20
Woodpecker, Workbook 4, Page 7

'pl' Cloze and Phonic Activities, Book 6, Pages 3–5
Ginn 360, Duplicating Masters, Level 5, Sheets 13, 14
Phonic Links, Book 3, Worksheets 4, 18
Read Write and Spell, Book 2, Pages 19, 20
Sound Practice, Book 4, Page 8
Soundstart Phonic Workshop 2
Woodpecker, Workbook 4, Page 8

'sl' Cloze and Phonic Activities, Book 6, Pages 21–23
Read Write and Spell, Stage 2, Pages 19, 20
Phonic Links, Book 3, Worksheets 4
Sound Practice, Book 4, Page 9
Soundstart Phonic Workshop 2
Woodpecker, Workbook 4, Page 8

Initial Consonant Blend with 'r' General

Active Phonics, Workbook 4
Cloze and Phonic Activities, Book 5
Fuzzbuzz, Letters Book 2, Page 32
Phonic Blending, Book 2, Lesson 11
Phonics – Resource Bank and Teachers' Guide Sheet, D1, D4
The Phonics Book (Stanley Thornes)
Young Shorty Activity Book 1, Pages 21, 22
Sound Practice, Book 4, Pages 14, 19–23
SRA Schoolhouse, Rose, Card 1
Woodpecker, Workbook 5, Pages 3, 4

'br' Crosswords 2
Learning Phonics 2, Cassette 2
Phonic Links Book 3, Worksheets 4
Read Write and Spell, Stage 2, Pages 19, 20
Sound Practice, Book 4, Page 11
Soundstart Phonic Workshop 2
Woodpecker, Workbook 4, Page 4

'cr' Crosswords 2
Learning Phonics 2, Cassette 2
Phonic Links, Book 3, Worksheets 4, 11
Read Write and Spell, Stage 2, Pages 19, 20
Sound Practice, Book 4, Page 12
Soundstart Phonic Workshop 2
Woodpecker, Workbook 4, Page 4

'dr' Crosswords 2
Ginn 360, Duplicating Masters, Level 7, Sheet 6
Learning Phonics 2, Cassette 2
Phonic Links, Book 3, Worksheets 6, 18
Read Write and Spell, Stage 2, Pages 19, 20
Sound Practice, Book 4, Page 13
Sound Sense, Book 6, Page 11
Soundstart Phonic Workshop 2
Woodpecker, Workbook 4, Page 5

'fr' Ginn 360, Duplicating Masters, Level 5, Sheets 11, 14
Phonic Links, Book 3, Worksheets 4
Sound, Patterns and Words, Book 4, Page 8
Sure-fire Phonics, Book 5, Page 25
Woodpecker, Workbook 4, Page 6
Ginn 360, Duplicating Masters, Level 5, Sheet 16

'gr' Phonic Links, Book 3, Worksheets 14, 38
Sound Practice, Book 4, Page 16
Sound Sense, Book 6, Pages 16, 17 (O/P)
Soundstart Phonic Workshop 2
Woodpecker, Workbook 4, Page 6

'pr' Cloze and Phonic Activities, Book 6, Pages 6–8
Crosswords 2
Learning Phonics 2, Cassette 2
Phonic Links, Book 3, Worksheets 14, 18
Read Write and Spell, Stage 2, Pages 19, 20
Sound Practice, Book 4, Page 17
Spelling Patterns, Practice Sheet 67
Woodpecker, Workbook 4, Page 6

'tr' Cloze and Phonic Activities, Book 7, Pages 24–26
Ginn 360, Duplicating Masters, Level 5, Sheets 11, 14
Phonic Links, Book 3, Worksheet 11
Read Write and Spell, Stage 2, Pages 19, 20
Sound Practice, Book 4, Page 18
Sound Sense, Book 6, Pages 8, 9 (O/P)
Soundstart Phonic Workshop 2
Woodpecker, Workbook 4, Page 5

Other Initial   **'sc'** Cloze and Phonic Activities, Book 6, Pages 12–14
Consonant Blends   Crosswords 2

Learning Phonics 2, Cassette 3
Phonic Links, Book 3, Worksheets 6
The Phonics Book (Stanley Thornes)
Sounds and Words, Book 4, Page 1
Sound Practice, Book 5, Pages 8, 12
Woodpecker, Workbook 4, Page 10

'sk'   Cloze and Phonic Activities, Book 6, Pages 18–20
Phonic Bank, Card 19
The Phonics Book (Stanley Thornes)
Sound Practice, Book 5, Page 11
Soundstart Phonic Workshop 2
Sounds and Words, Book 4, Page 1
SRA Schoolhouse, Rose, Card 3
Sure-fire Phonics, Book 5, Page 3
Woodpecker, Workbook 4, Pages 12, 14

'sm'   Cloze and Phonic Activities, Book 6, Pages 24-26
Ginn 360, Duplicating Masters, Level 6, Sheet 7
Phonic Bank, Card 19
Phonic Links, Book 3, Worksheets 14, 18
The Phonics Book (Stanley Thornes)
Read Write and Spell, Book 2, Pages 19, 20
Sound Practice, Book 5, Pages 6, 11
Sounds and Words, Book 4, Page 7
Sure-fire Phonics, Book 5, Page 6
Woodpecker, Workbook 4, Page 9

'sn'   Cloze and Phonic Activities, Book 6, Pages 27–29
Phonic Bank, Card 19
Phonic Links, Book 3, Worksheet 38
The Phonics Book (Stanley Thornes)
Read Write and Spell, Book 2, Pages 19, 20
Sound Practice, Book 5, Pages 9, 12
Soundstart Phonic Workshop 2
Sounds and Words, Book 4, Page 7
Sure-fire Phonics, Book 5, Page 8
Woodpecker, Workbook 4, Page 10

'sp'   Cloze and Phonic Activities, Book 7, Pages 3–5
Crossword 16
Learning Phonics 1, Cassette 4
Phonic Bank, Card 18
Phonic Links, Book 3, Worksheets 4, 11
The Phonics Book (Stanley Thornes)
SRA Schoolhouse, Rose, Card 3
Sound Practice, Book 5, Pages 5, 11
Soundstart Phonic Workshop 2
Tree Worksheet 16
Woodpecker, Workbook 4, Pages 9, 14

'st'   Breaking the Code, Book 2
        Cloze and Phonic Activities, Book 7, Pages 15–17
        Crossword 14
        Fuzzbuzz, Letters Book 2, Pages 4, 6
        Learning Phonics 1, Cassette 4
        New Phonic Blending 3
        Phonic Bank, Card 18
        Phonic Links, Book 3, Worksheets 4, 14
        The Phonics Book (Stanley Thornes)
        Read Write and Spell, Book 2, Pages 19, 20
        Sound Practice, Book 5, Pages 3, 12
        Sound Sense, Book 5, Pages 8, 9 (O/P)
        Soundstart Phonic Workshop 2
        SRA Schoolhouse, Rose, Card 3
        Tree Workshop 14
        Woodpecker, Workbook 4, Pages 9, 14

'sw'   Cloze and Phonic Activities, Book 7, Pages 21–23
        Crosswords 2
        Learning Phonics 2, Cassette 3
        Phonic Bank, Card 19
        Phonic Links, Book 3, Worksheets 38
        The Phonics Book (Stanley Thornes)
        Sound Practice, Book 5, Pages 10, 11
        SRA Schoolhouse, Rose, Card 3
        Woodpecker, Workbook 5, Page 10

'squ'   Cloze and Phonic Activities, Book 7, Pages 12–14
        Ginn 360, Duplicating Masters, Level 8, Sheet 18
        Phonic Blending, Book 3, Lesson 10
        Phonics – Resource Bank and Teachers' Guide Sheet P6
        Woodpecker, Workbook 8, Pages 1, 2

'tw'   Cloze and Phonic Activities, Book 7, Pages 27–29
        Ginn 360, Duplicating Masters, Level 7, Sheet 10
        Phonic Bank, Card 20
        Sounds and Words, Book 4, Page 8

Initial Consonant   Active Phonics, Workbook 5
Blend Revision   Alpha to Omega, Stage 1, Pages 31–33
                            Flying Boot – Phonic Book 4
                            Fuzzbuzz, Letters Book 2, Pages 22–24
                            Key Phonics, Book 2, Pages 18–24
                            Phonic Bank PCM 4
                            Phonic Blending, Book 2, Lessons 14, 15, 17, 19
                            Phonic Fold-Ups
                            Phonics – Resource Bank and Teachers' Guide Sheets D2, D4
                            Young Shorty Activity Book 1, Pages 23, 27, 28
                            SRA Schoolhouse, Rose, Cards 4, 5
                            Stile Phonics Book 3, Pages 1–4, 7–16
                                            Book 4, Pages 2, 9

Book 5, Pages 2, 10–12
Book 6, Pages 4, 5, 7, 8, 11, 16
Book 7, Pages 2, 7, 10, 12, 14, 16
Book 8, Pages 2, 4, 7, 9, 10, 12, 14
Stile Phonic Practice Card 16
Supersonics, Reading Books Set 3

Long Initial Consonant Blends

'scr' Cloze and Phonic Activities, Book 6, Pages 15–17
Phonic Bank, Card 45
Phonic Blending, Book 3, Lesson 9
Phonic Links, Book 3, Worksheet 11
Phonics – Resource Bank and Teachers' Guide Sheets F3, F4
Sounds and Words, Book 4, Page 1
Woodpecker, Workbook 8, Pages 3, 4

'str' Cloze and Phonic Activities, Book 7, Pages 18–20
Phonic Bank, Card 45
Phonic Links, Book 3, Worksheet 14
Phonic Blending, Book 3, Lesson 1, 4
Phonics – Resource Bank and Teachers' Guide Sheets F1, F2
Woodpecker, Workbook 8, Pages 1, 24

'spl' Cloze and Phonic Activities, Book 7, Pages 6–8
Phonic Blending, Book 3, Lesson 8
Phonic Links, Book 3, Worksheet 6
Phonics – Resource Bank and Teachers' Guide Sheets F3, F4
Woodpecker, Workbook 8, Pages 5, 6

'spr' Cloze and Phonic Activities, Book 7, Pages 9–11
Phonic Bank, Card 45
Phonic Blending, Book 3, Lesson 6
Phonic Links, Book 3, Worksheet 38
Phonics – Resource Bank and Teachers' Guide Sheets F3, F4

Long Initial Consonant Blend Revision

Ginn 360, Duplicating Masters, Level 7, Sheet 23
SRA Schoolhouse, Rose, Cards 11, 12

Vowel Digraphs

'ai' Crossword 11
Finger Phonics, Book 4
First Vowel Digraph Book
Flying Boot – Phonic Book 3
Fuzzbuzz, Letters Book 4, Pages 12–16
Ginn 360, Duplicating Masters, Level 7, Sheet 22
Key Phonics, Book 3, Pages 14, 16
Learning Phonics 1, Cassette 3
New Phonic Blending 4
Phonic Bank, Card 25
Phonic Blending, Book 2, Lesson 10
Phonic Links, Book 3, Worksheets 1, 4
The Phonics Book (Stanley Thornes)
Phonic Workshop, Card 7
The Phonics Handbook

Phonics – Resource Bank and Teachers' Guide Sheets B3, B4, H1
Read Write and Spell, Book 2, Pages 18, 19
                                  Book 3, Pages 18, 19
Reading Quest 4, Pages 20, 21 (O/P)
Young Shorty Activity Book 2, Page 15
Sound Practice, Book 5, Page 18
Sound Sense, Book 7, Pages 2, 4–6 (O/P)
Soundstart Phonic Workshop 2
Sounds and Words, Book 3, Page 13
SRA Schoolhouse, Orange, Card 17
Stile Phonics, Book 10, Pages 9, 11, 12
Sure-fire Phonics, Book 6, Page 8
Tree Worksheet 10

'al' (talk)   Phonic Bank, Card 28
Phonic Workshop, Card 41
Phonics – Resource Bank and Teachers' Guide Sheet H2
Soundstart Phonic Workshop 2

'ar'   Breaking the Code, Book 3
Crossword 17
Finger Phonics, Book 7
First Vowel Digraph Book
Flying Boot – Phonic Book 3
Fuzzbuzz, Letters Book 3, Pages 43–47
Ginn 360, Duplicating Masters, Level 6, Sheets 18, 19
                                  Level 9, Sheet 14
Learning Phonics 1, Cassette 5
New Phonic Blending 4
Phonic Bank, Card 23
Phonic Links Book 3, Worksheet 30
Phonic Workshop, Card 3
The Phonics Book (Stanley Thornes)
The Phonics Handbook
Phonics – Resource Bank and Teachers' Guide, Sheets K1, K3, K4
Read Write and Spell, Book 4, Page 31
Sound Practice, Book 5, Page 21
Sound Sense, Book 4, Page 12 (O/P)
Soundstart Phonic Workshop 2
Sounds and Words, Book 4, Page 12
SRA Schoolhouse, Yellow, Card 1
Stile Phonics, Book 11, Pages 1, 2, 16
Sure-fire Phonics, Book 6, Page 11
Tree Worksheet 17
Woodpecker, Workbook 9, Pages 3, 4

(warm)   Sounds and Words, Book 5, Page 21

'au'   Active Phonics, Workbooks 5 and 6
Ginn 360, Duplicating Masters, Level 8, Sheet 20
                                  Level 9, Sheet 9

Key Phonics, Book 4, Page 15
Phonic Bank, Card 27
Phonic Links, Book 3, Worksheet 35
Phonic Workshop, Card 44
Phonics – Resource Bank and Teachers' Guide Sheets P1, P2, P3
Read Write and Spell, Book 3, Page 32
Reading Quest 4, Pages 42, 43 (O/P)
Sound Sense, Book 7, Page 39 (O/P)
Sounds and Words, Book 5, Page 15
Spelling Patterns, Practice Sheet 40
Stile Phonics, Book 11, Pages 15, 16
Sure-fire Phonics, Book 6, Page 17

'aw'   Active Phonics, Workbook 6
Crosswords 2
Fuzzbuzz, Letters Book 4, Pages 33–36
Ginn 360, Duplicating Masters, Level 6, Sheet 22
                                             Level 9, Sheet 9
Key Phonics, Book 3, Page 38
Learning Phonics 2, Cassette 4
Language 1, Copymaster C73
Phonic Bank, Card 27
Phonic Ladders
Phonic Links, Book 3, Worksheet 35
Phonic Workshop, Card 43
The Phonics Book (Stanley Thornes)
Phonics – Resource Bank and Teachers' Guide, Sheets K7, K8
Read Write and Spell, Book 3, Page 32
Reading Quest 4, Pages 38, 39 (O/P)
The Second Vowel Digraph Book
Sound Practice, Book 5, Page 20
Sound Sense, Book 7, Page 39 (O/P)
Soundstart Phonic Workshop 2
Sounds and Words, Book 5, Page 16
Spelling Patterns, Practice Sheet 31
Stile Phonics, Book 11, Pages 9, 10, 15, 16
Sure-fire Phonics, Book 6, Page 18
Woodpecker, Workbook 8, Pages 12, 13

'ay'   Active Phonics, Workbook 5
Crosswords 2
Fuzzbuzz, Letters Book 3, Pages 28–32
Ginn 360, Duplicating Sheets, Level 6, Sheet 6
Key Phonics, Book 3, Pages 32, 33
Learning Phonics 2, Cassette 4
Language 1, Copymaster C64
Phonic Bank, Card 25
Phonic Ladders
Phonic Links, Book 3, Worksheets 2, 4
Phonic Workshop, Card 6
The Phonics Book (Stanley Thornes)

Phonics – Resource Bank and Teachers' Guide, Sheet B4
Read Write and Spell, Book 3, Pages 18, 19
Reading Quest 4, Pages 18, 19 (O/P)
The Second Vowel Digraph Book
Young Shorty Activity Book 2, Page 16
Sound Practice, Book 5, Page 19
Sound Sense, Book 7, Pages 2, 4–6 (O/P)
Soundstart Phonic Workshop 2
Sounds and Words, Book 3, Page 12
SRA Schoolhouse, Orange, Card 17
Sure-fire Phonics, Book 6, Page 9
Woodpecker, Workbook 1, Page 8
Woodpecker, Workbook 6, Pages 11–13

'ea' (eat)   Active Phonics, Workbook 5
Breaking the Code, Book 3
Crosswords 2
First Vowel Digraph Book
Fuzzbuzz, Letters Book 3, Pages 33–37
Ginn 360, Duplicating Masters, Level 5, Sheets 8, 9
                    Level 9, Sheet 12
Key Phonics, Book 3, Page 15, 16
Learning Phonics 2, Cassette 5
Language 1, Copymaster C63
New Phonic Blending 4
Phonic Bank, Card 21
Phonic Blending, Book 2, Lesson 4
Phonic Links, Book 3, Worksheets 10, 11, 17, 18
Phonic Workshop, Card 35
The Phonics Book (Stanley Thornes)
Phonics – Resource Bank and Teachers' Guide, Sheet B5, B6, B8
Read Write and Spell, Stage 3, Pages 14, 15
Reading Quest 4, Pages 16, 17 (O/P)
Young Shorty Activity Book 1, Pages 12, 13
Sound Practice, Book 5, Page 15
Sound Sense, Book 6, Pages 31, 33, 34, 37 (O/P)
Soundstart Phonic Workshop 2
Sounds and Words, Book 2, Page 6
SRA Schoolhouse, Yellow, Cards 6, 9, 10
Stile Phonics, Book 9, Pages 8, 9, 11–15
Supersonics, Reading Books Set 4
Sure-fire Phonics, Book 6, Page 6
Woodpecker, Workbook 6, Pages 7–9

(head)   Active Phonics, Workbook 5
Ginn 360, Duplicating Masters, Level 8, Sheet 11
Key Phonics, Book 3, Page 29
New Phonic Blending 4
Phonic Bank, Card 21
Phonic Links, Book 3, Worksheets 10, 11
Phonic Workshop, Card 36
Phonics – Resource Bank and Teachers' Guide, Sheets L10, L11

Read Write and Spell, Stage 3, Page 48
Reading Quest 4, Pages 22, 23 (O/P)
The Second Vowel Digraph Book
Sound Sense, Book 6, Pages 35, 37 (O/P)
Soundstart Phonic Workshop 2
Sounds and Words, Book 4, Page 17
Sure-fire Phonics, Book 6, Page 7
Spelling Patterns, Practice Sheet 21
SRA Schoolhouse, Yellow, Card 6, 9, 10
Supersonics, Reading Books Set 4
Woodpecker, Workbook 6, Pages 10, 12, 13

'ee'   Active Phonics, Workbook 5
Breaking the Code, Book 2
Crossword 9
Finger Phonics, Book 4
First Vowel Digraph Book
Flying Boot – Phonic Book 3
Fuzzbuzz, Letters Book 3, Pages 18–22
Ginn 360, Duplicating Masters, Level 5, Sheets 6, 7, 9
                                        Level 9, Sheet 12
Key Phonics, Book 3, Page 6
Learning Phonic 1, Cassette 3
New Phonic Blending 4
Phonic Bank, Card 21
Phonic Blending, Book 2, Lesson 2
Phonic Ladders
Phonic Workshop, Card 2
The Phonics Book (Stanley Thornes)
The Phonics Handbook
Phonics – Resource Bank and Teachers' Guide, Sheets B7, B8
Read Write and Spell, Stage 2, Page 10
Reading Quest 4, Pages 4, 5 (O/P)
Young Shorty Activity Book 2, Page 2
Sound Practice, Book 5, Page 14
Sound Sense, Book 2, Pages 2–5 (O/P)
Soundstart Phonic Workshop 2
SRA Schoolhouse, Orange, Card 18
Stile Phonics Book, Pages 8, 10–15
Supersonics, Reading Books Set 4
Sure-fire Phonics, Book 6, Pages 2, 5
Tree Worksheet 8
Woodpecker, Workbook 6, Pages 2, 4, 5

'ei'   Ginn 360, Duplicating Masters, Level 9, Sheet 12
Read Write and Spell, Stage 4, Page 24
Reading Quest 5, Pages 6, 7 (O/P)
Spelling Patterns, Practice Sheet 35
SRA Schoolhouse, Orange, Card 17

'er'   Active Phonics, Workbook 6
Finger Phonics, Book 7

67

Fuzzbuzz, Letters Book 3, Pages 3–7
Ginn 360, Duplicating Masters, Level 7, Sheets 13, 14
                              Level 9, Sheet 14
Language 1, Copymaster C69
New Phonic Blending 4
Phonic Bank, Card 22
Phonic Links, Book 3, Worksheet 31
Phonic Workshop, Card 20
The Phonics Book (Stanley Thornes)
The Phonics Handbook
Phonics – Resource Bank and Teachers' Guide, Sheets J4, J5
Read Write and Spell, Stage 3, Page 4
The Second Vowel Digraph Book
Sound Practice, Book 5, Page 27
Sound Sense, Book 4, Pages 8, 9
                        Book 8, Page 10 (O/P)
Soundstart Phonic Workshop 2
Sounds and Words, Book 2, Page 11
SRA Schoolhouse, Yellow, Card 2
Stile Phonics, Book 11, Pages 7, 8, 16
Sure-fire Phonics, Book 6, Page 12
Woodpecker, Workbook 9, Page 1

'ew'   Active Phonics, Workbook 6
Crosswords 2
Flying Boot – Phonic Book 4
Ginn 360, Duplicating Masters, Level 7, Sheet 8
Key Phonics, Book 3, Page 39
Learning Phonics 2, Cassette 4
Phonic Links, Book 3, Worksheets 37, 38
Phonic Workshop, Card 16
The Phonics Book (Stanley Thornes)
Phonics – Resource Bank and Teachers' Guide, Sheets J6, J7
Read Write and Spell, Stage 3, Pages 42, 43
Reading Quest 4, Pages 46, 47 (O/P)
The Second Vowel Digraph Book
Sound Sense, Book 8, Page 13 (O/P)
Soundstart Phonic Workshop 2
Sounds and Words, Book 5, Page 13
Spelling Patterns, Practice Sheet 28
Stile Phonics, Book 10, Pages 14–16
Sure-fire Phonics, Book 6, Page 29

'ey'   Read Write and Spell, Stage 4, Pages 12, 13
The Second Vowel Digraph Book
Spelling Patterns, Practice Sheet 38
SRA Schoolhouse, Orange, Card 18

'ie'   Active Phonics, Workbook 5
Finger Phonics, Book 4
Ginn 360, Duplicating Masters, Level 8, Sheets 5, 6
                        Level 9, Sheet 12

Key Phonics, Book 3, Page 40
Phonic Bank, Card 34
Phonic Links, Book 3, Worksheets 36, 411
Phonic Workshop, Card 32
The Phonics Book (Stanley Thornes)
The Phonics Handbook
Phonics – Resource Bank and Teachers' Guide, Sheet L12
Read Write and Spell, Stage 4, Page 18
Reading Quest 5, Pages 4, 5 (O/P)
The Second Vowel Digraph Book
Sound Sense, Book 8, Pages 27 (O/P)
Sounds and Words, Book 6, Page 23
Spelling Patterns, Practice Sheets 34, 44
Stile Phonics, Book 10, Pages 1–4
Sure-fire Phonics, Book 6, Page 27

'ir'   Active Phonics, Workbook 6
First Vowel Digraph Book
Crossword 18
Fuzzbuzz, Letters Book 4, Pages 37–40
Ginn 360, Duplicating Masters, Level 7, Sheets 13, 14
Learning Phonics 1, Cassette 5
New Phonic Blending 4
Phonic Bank, Card 22
Phonic Workshop, Card 21
Phonic Links, Book 3, Worksheet 33
Phonics – Resource Bank and Teachers' Guide, Sheet J5
The Phonics Book (Stanley Thornes)
The Phonics Handbook
Read Write and Spell, Stage 3, Page 12
Young Shorty, Activity Book 2, Page 31
Sound Sense, Book 8, Pages 10, 12 (O/P)
Soundstart Phonic Workshop 2
Sounds and Words, Book 3, Page 17
SRA Schoolhouse, Yellow, Card 2
Stile Phonics, Book 11, Pages 12, 16
Sure-fire Phonics, Book 6, Page 13
Tree Worksheet 18
Woodpecker, Workbook 9, Pages 5, 6

'oa'   Active Phonics, Workbook 6
Breaking the Code, Book 2
Crossword 12
Finger Phonics, Book 4
First Vowel Digraph Book
Fuzzbuzz, Letters Book 4, Pages 18–22
Ginn 360, Duplicating Masters, Level 7, Sheets 15, 17
Key Phonics, Book 3, Page 12
Learning Phonics 1, Cassette 3
Language 1, Copymaster C70
New Phonic Blending 4
Phonic Bank, Card 23

Phonic Blending, Book 2, Lesson 8
Phonic Ladders
Phonic Links, Book 3, Worksheets 5, 6
Phonics – Resource Bank and Teachers' Guide, Sheet C4, C5
The Phonics Book (Stanley Thornes)
Phonic Workshop, Card 10
Read Write and Spell, Stage 3, Page 22
Reading Quest 4, Pages 30, 31 (O/P)
Sound Practice, Book 5, Page 16
Sound Sense, Book 7, Pages 32, 33 (O/P)
Soundstart Phonic Workshop 2
Sounds and Words, Book 4, Page 5
SRA Schoolhouse, Orange, Card 19
Stile Phonics, Book 10, Pages 6–8
Sure-fire Phonics, Book 6, Page 23
Tree Worksheet 11
Woodpecker, Workbook 8, Pages 8, 9

'oe'   Key Phonics, Book 4, Page 10
The Second Vowel Digraph Book
Spelling Patterns, Practice Sheet 45
SRA Schoolhouse, Orange, Card 19
Sure-fire Phonics, Book 6, Page 29

'oi'   Active Phonics, Workbook 6
Crosswords 2
Finger Phonics, Book 7
Ginn 360, Duplicating Masters, Level 8, Sheet 13
Key Phonics, Book 3, Page 27
Learning Phonics 2, Cassette 4
Language 1, Copymaster C74
Phonic Bank, Card 26
Phonics – Resource Bank and Teachers' Guide, Sheets L1, L2, L4
The Phonics Book (Stanley Thornes)
Phonic Workshop, Card 26
The Phonics Handbook
Read Write and Spell, Stage 3, Page 26
Reading Quest 4, Pages 32, 33 (O/P)
The Second Vowel Digraph Book
Sound Sense, Book 7, Pages 12, 14 (O/P)
Soundstart Phonic Workshop 2
Sounds and Words, Book 4, Page 18
Spelling Patterns, Practice Sheet 33
SRA Schoolhouse, Yellow, Card 13
Stile Phonics, Book 11, Pages 5, 6, 16
Sure-fire Phonics, Book 6, Page 19
Woodpecker, Workbook 8, Pages 12, 13

'oo' (pool)   Active Phonics, Workbook 5
Breaking the Code, Book 2
Crossword 10

Finger Phonics, Book 5
Flying Boot – Phonic Book 4
Ginn 360, Duplicating Masters, Level 6, Sheet 17
Key Phonics, Book 3, Page 27
Learning Phonics 1, Cassette 3
Language 1, Copymaster C62
New Phonic Blending 4
Phonic Bank, Card 33
Phonic Blending, Book 1, Lesson 18
Phonic Ladders
The Phonics Handbook
Phonics – Resource Bank and Teachers' Guide, Sheets J1–J3
Read Write and Spell, Stage 2, Page 14
Reading Quest 4, Pages 6, 7 (O/P)
Sound Practice, Book 5, Page 13
Sound Sense, Book 2, Pages 6–8 (O/P)
Soundstart Phonic Workshop 2
SRA Schoolhouse, Yellow, Card 8–10
Stiles Phonics, Book 10, Pages 10, 13, 16
Sure-fire Phonics, Book 6, Pages 3–5
Tree Worksheet 9
Woodpecker, Workbook 1, Page 10
Woodpecker, Workbook 6, Pages 6, 8, 9

(book)   Active Phonics, Workbook 5
Finger Phonics, Book 5
First Vowel Digraph Book
Fuzzbuzz, Letters Book 3, Pages 8–12
Ginn 360, Duplicating Masters, Level 6, Sheet 16
New Phonic Blending 4
Phonic Bank, Card 33
Phonic Blending, Book 2, Lesson 4
Phonic Workshop, Card 1
The Phonics Book (Stanley Thornes)
The Phonics Handbook
Phonics – Resource Bank and Teachers' Guide, Sheets J1–J3
Read Write and Spell, Stage 2, Page 14
Reading Quest 4, Pages 6, 7 (O/P)
Young Shorty Activity Book 2, Pages 3, 4
Soundstart Phonic Workshop 2
Spelling Patterns, Practice Sheet 17
SRA Schoolhouse, Yellow, Cards 8–10
Sure-fire Phonics, Book 6, Pages 4, 5
Woodpecker, Workbook 6, Pages 11–13

'or'   Active Phonics, Workbook 6
Breaking the Code, Book 3
Crossword 19
Finger Phonics, Book 4
Fuzzbuzz, Letters Book 4, Pages 7–11
Ginn 360, Duplicating Masters, Level 7, Sheets 11, 12
                                    Level 9, Sheet 14

Learning Phonic Cassette 5, Side 2
Language 1, Copymaster C72
New Phonic Blending 4
Phonic Bank, Card 27
Phonic Blending, Book 2, Lesson 20
Phonic Links, Book 3, Worksheet 31
Phonic Workshop, Card 42
The Phonics Book (Stanley Thornes)
The Phonics Handbook
Phonics – Resource Bank and Teachers' Guide, Sheets K5, K6
Read Write and Spell, Stage 2, Page 54
                  Stage 4, Page 32
Sound Practice, Book 5, Page 22
Sound Sense, Book 4, Pages 14, 15
Soundstart Phonic Workshop 2
Sound and Words, Book 4, Page 13
Spelling Practice, Sheet 18
SRA Schoolhouse, Yellow, Card 1
Stile Phonics, Book 1, Pages 1, 2, 8, 16
Sure-fire Phonics, Book 6, Page 14
Tree Worksheet 19
Woodpecker, Workbook 9, Pages 5, 6

(word)   Sounds and Words, Book 5, Page 21

   'ou'   Active Phonics, Workbook 6
Crosswords 2
Finger Phonics, Book 7
Fuzzbuzz, Letters Book 3, Pages 38–42
Ginn 360, Duplicating Masters, Level 7, Sheets 18, 20
                                 Level 8, Sheet 17
                                 Level 9, Sheets 10, 11
Key Phonics, Book 3, Page 28
Language 1, Copymaster C67
New Phonic Blending 4
Phonic Bank, Card 24
Phonic Blending, Book 2, Lesson 16
Phonic Links, Book 3, Worksheets 12, 13, 14, 21
Phonic Workshop, Card 13
The Phonics Book (Stanley Thornes)
The Phonics Handbook
Phonics – Resource Bank and Teachers' Guide, Sheets R3, R4, L8, L9
Read Write and Spell, Stage 3, Page 38
Reading Quest, Book 4, Pages 26, 27 (O/P)
Sound Practice, Book 5, Page 17
Sound Sense, Book 7, Pages 18, 23–24
Soundstart Phonic Workshop 2
Sounds and Words, Book 3, Page 4
SRA Schoolhouse, Yellow, Card 11
Stile Phonics, Book 11, Pages 3, 4, 16
Sure-fire Phonics, Book 6, Page 22

Woodpecker, Workbook 1, Page 9
Woodpecker, Workbook 8, Pages 10, 11

'ow' (snow)   Active Phonics, Workbook 6
Ginn 360, Duplicating Masters, Level 7, Sheets 16, 17, 21
Key Phonics, Book 4, Page 3
Language 1, Copymaster C71
Phonic Bank, Card 24
Phonic Blending, Book 2, Lesson 12
Phonic Links, Book 3, Worksheets 24–27
The Phonics Book (Stanley Thornes)
Phonics – Resource Bank and Teachers' Guide, Sheets L5, L7
Read Write and Spell, Stage 2, Page 28
                    Stage 3, Page 22
Reading Quest 4, Pages 28, 29 (O/P)
The Second Vowel Digraph Book
Sound Sense, Book 7, Page 26 (O/P)
Sounds and Words, Book 3, Page 5
SRA Schoolhouse, Yellow, Cards 7, 9, 10
Stile Phonics, Book 10, Pages 5, 7, 8
Sure-fire Phonics, Book 6, Page 25
Woodpecker, Workbook 8, Pages 10, 11

(cow)   Active Phonics, Workbook 6
Breaking the Code, Book 3
First Vowel Digraph Book
Ginn 360, Duplicating Masters, Level 7, Sheets 3, 20, 21
Key Phonics, Book 3, Page 11
Language 1, Copymasters C65, C66
New Phonic Blending 4
Phonic Bank, Card 24
Phonic Workshop, Card 12
Phonic Links, Book 3, Worksheets 24–27
The Phonics Book (Stanley Thornes)
Phonics – Resource Bank and Teachers' Guide, Sheets L6, L7
Reading Quest, Book 4, Pages 24, 25 (O/P)
Sound Practice, Book 12, Page 23
Sound Sense, Book 7, Pages 22–24 (O/P)
Soundstart Phonic Workshop 2
Sounds and Words, Book 4, Page 7
Spelling Patterns, Practice Sheet 15
SRA Schoolhouse, Yellow, Cards 7, 9, 10, 11
Sure-fire Phonics, Book 6, Page 24
Woodpecker, Workbook 8, Pages 8, 9

'oy'   Active Phonics, Workbook 6
Ginn 360, Duplicating Masters, Level 8, Sheet 13
Key Phonics, Book 3, Page 37
Phonic Bank, Card 26
Phonic Workshop, Card 25
The Phonics Book (Stanley Thornes)

Phonics – Resource Bank and Teachers' Guide, Sheets L3, L4
Read Write and Spell, Stage 3, Page 26
The Second Vowel Digraph Book
Reading Quest 4, Pages 34, 35 (O/P)
Sound Sense, Book 7, Pages 12, 14 (O/P)
Sounds and Words, Book 4, Page 18
Spelling Patterns, Practice Sheet 32
SRA Schoolhouse, Yellow, Card 13
Stile Phonics, Book 11, Pages 5, 6
Sure-fire Phonics, Book 6, Page 20
Woodpecker, Workbook 8, Pages 14, 15

'ue' Finger Phonics, Book 7
Key Phonics, Book 4, Page 11
Phonic Workshop, Card 17
The Phonics Handbook (Stanley Thornes)
Phonics – Resource Bank and Teachers' Guide, Sheet L12
Reading Quest, Book 4, Pages 44, 45 (O/P)
The Second Vowel Digraph Book
Spelling Patterns, Practice Sheet 45
Sure-fire Phonics, Book 6, Page 29

'ui' Phonics - Resource Bank and Teachers' Guide, Sheet L12
The Second Vowel Digraph Book
Spelling Patterns, Practice Sheet 47

'ur' Active Phonics, Workbook 6
Fuzzbuzz, Letters Book 4, Pages 23–25
Ginn 360, Duplicating Masters, Level 7, Sheets 13, 14
Language 1, Copymaster C75
New Phonic Blending 4
Phonic Bank, Card 22
Phonic Blending, Book 2, Lesson 18
Phonic Links, Book 3, Worksheet 33
Phonic Workshop, Card 22
The Phonics Book (Stanley Thornes)
Phonics – Resource Bank and Teachers' Guide, Sheet J5
Read Write and Spell, Stage 3, Pages 21, 22
Young Shorty Activity Book 2, Page 30
Sound Sense, Book 8, Page 11 (O/P)
Soundstart Phonic Workshop 2
Sounds and Words, Book 3, Page 18
Spelling Patterns, Practice Sheet 29
SRA Schoolhouse, Yellow, Card 2
Stile Phonics, Book 11, Pages 11, 12, 16
Sure-fire Phonics, Book 6, Page 15
Woodpecker, Workbook 9, Pages 3, 4

Final 'y' Active Phonics, Workbook 5
Crosswords 2
Ginn 360, Duplicating Masters, Level 8, Sheets 3, 4

Key Phonics, Book 3, Page 34
              Book 4, Page 2
Phonic Bank, Card 35
Phonic Links, Book 3, Worksheet 41
Phonic Workshop, Cards 30, 31
Read Write and Spell, Stage 2, Page 20
Reading Quest 3, Pages 8–11 (O/P)
Reading Quest 5, Page 39 (O/P)
Sound Practice, Book 4, Page 31
Sound Sense, Book 6, Pages 20, 23 (O/P)
Soundstart, Phonic Workshop 2
Sounds and Words, Book 4, Page 19
Spelling Patterns, Practice Sheet 1
SRA Schoolhouse, Orange, Card 12
Stile Phonics, Book 10, Pages 1, 10–12
Sure-fire Phonics, Book 2, Pages 25, 26
Woodpecker, Workbook 8, Pages 14, 15

Prefixes, Word Beginnings

'be'   New Phonic Blending 5, 6
Reading Quest 5, Page 24 (O/P)
Sound Sense, Book 7, Page 7 (O/P)

'de'   New Phonic Blending 5
Reading Quest 5, Page 24 (O/P)
Sounds and Words, Book 6, Page 22

'dis'   New Phonic Blending 5, 6
Sound Sense, Book 8, Page 45 (O/P)

'pre'   New Phonic Blending 5, 6
Reading Quest 5, Page 25 (O/P)
Sounds and Words, Book 6, Page 21

're'   New Phonic Blending 5, 6
Sounds and Words, Book 6, Page 21
Sound Sense, Book 8, Page 45 (O/P)
Reading Quest 5, Page 25 (O/P)

Suffixes, endings

'ed'   Active Phonics, Workbook 6
Fuzzbuzz, Letters Book 4, Pages 41–47
Ginn 360, Duplicating Masters, Level 6, Sheets 1, 4
Language 1, Copymaster C46
New Phonic Blending 5, 6
Phonic Bank, Card 37
Phonic Links, Book 3, Worksheet 28
Read Write and Spell, Stage 2, Pages 56–58
Reading Quest 3, Pages 18, 19 (O/P)
Sound Sense, Book 4, Pages 26, 27
              Book 7, Page 7 (O/P)
Sounds and Words, Book 2, Pages 2, 8
SRA Schoolhouse, Green, Card 7

Woodpecker, Workbook 1, Page 14
Woodpecker, Workbook 7, Pages 2, 3, 8, 10, 12, 14, 16

'er'   New Phonic Blending 5, 6
Sound Sense, Book 4, Pages 8, 9
        Book 5, Pages 14, 15 (O/P)

'est'   New Phonic Blending 5
Sound Sense, Book 5, Pages 14, 15
        Book 8, Page 3 (O/P)

'ght'   Active Phonics, Workbook 5
Phonic Blending, Book 3, Lessons 2, 3
Stile Phonics, Book 8, Pages 5, 11
        Book 10, Pages 2–4
Tree Worksheet 4

'ful'   Ginn 360, Duplicating Masters, Level 8, Sheet 19
New Phonic Blending 5, 6
Specific Learning Difficulties Spelling Rules Book 1

'igh'   Active Phonics, Workbook 5
Crossword 3
Ginn 360, Duplicating Masters, Level 6, Sheet 23
Key Phonics, Book 4, Page 16
Learning Phonics 1, Cassette 1
Language 1, Copymaster C68
Phonic Bank, Card 34
Phonic Links, Book 3, Worksheet 39
Phonics – Resource Bank and Teachers' Guide, Sheet H3
The Phonics Book (Stanley Thornes)
Phonic Workshop, Card 29
Read Write and Spell, Stage 3, Pages 46, 47
Reading Quest 5, Page 3 (O/P)
Sounds and Words, Book 4, Page 20
Soundstart Phonic Workshop 2
Woodpecker, Workbook 7, Page 15

'ing'   Active Phonics, Workbook 6
Crossword 6
Ginn 360, Duplicating Masters, Level 6, Sheets 4, 5, 8, 9, 21,
        Level 5, Sheet 21
Learning Phonics 1, Cassette 2
New Phonic Blending 5, 6
Phonic Bank, Card 32
Phonic Links, Book 3, Worksheet 29
Phonics – Resource Bank and Teachers' Guide, Sheet 11
Reading Quest 3, Pages 16, 17 (O/P)
Sound Practice, Book 4, Page 31
Sound Sense, Book 5, Page 4
        Book 7, Page 7 (O/P)

Book 8, Page 45
Sounds and Words, Book 2, Page 1
Specific Learning Difficulties Spelling Rules Book 1
SRA Schoolhouse, Green, Card 7
Sure-fire Phonics, Book 4, Page 15
Tree Worksheet 6

'ion'   Active Phonics, Workbook 6
New Phonic Blending 5, 6
Phonic Bank, Card 46
Phonic Workshop, Cards 57, 58
Phonics – Resource Bank and Teachers' Guide, Sheets Q5, Q6
Read Write and Spell, Stage 4, Pages 11, 22, 23
Reading Quest 5, Pages 28, 29
Sound Sense, Book 8, Pages 29–33, 35 (O/P)
Sounds and Words, Book 6, Page 11
Spelling Patterns, Practice Sheet 43
Stile Phonics, Book 12, Page 16

'ious'   Reading Quest 5, Pages 31, 32 (O/P)
Sounds and Words, Book 6, Page 17

'le'   Fuzzbuzz, Letter Book 4, Pages 27–31
Ginn 360, Duplicating Masters, Level 8, Sheet 12
Key Phonics, Book 4, Page 8
Learning Phonics 1, Cassette 6
New Phonic Blending 5
Phonic Blending, Book 4, Lessons 10, 12
Phonic Links, Book 3, Worksheet 40
Phonics – Resource Bank and Teachers' Guide, Sheet J9
Sounds and Words, Book 2, Page 12
Specific Learning Difficulties Spelling Rules Book 1
Read Write and Spell, Stage 3, Pages 44, 45
Reading Quest, Pages 12, 13 (O/P)
Spelling Patterns, Practice Sheet 16
Stile Phonics, Book 7, Page 15
                Book 8, Pages 3, 5, 13, 15
Woodpecker, Workbook 9, Pages 10, 11

'less/ness'   Ginn 360, Duplicating Masters, Level 9, Sheet 19
New Phonic Blending 5
Sound Sense, Book 8, Page 43 (O/P)

'ly'   Ginn 360, Duplicating Masters, Level 8, Sheet 8
Phonics – Resource Bank and Teachers' Guide, Sheet I5
Read Write and Spell, Stage 4, Pages 15, 16
Sound Sense, Book 2, Page 29
                Book 5, Page 6 (O/P)

'ious'   Phonics – Resource Bank and Teachers' Guide, Sheet S1
Reading Quest 5, Page 30 (O/P)
Sounds and Words, Book 6, Page 17

'ure' Read Write and Spell, Stage 4, Pages 20, 39
Reading Quest 5, Page 33 (O/P)
Sounds and Words, Book 6, Page 17
Spelling Patterns, Practice Sheet 20
Stile Phonics, Book 12, Pages 11, 12

Soft 'c' Active Phonics, Workbook 6
Alpha to Omega, Stage 1, Pages 6a, 6b
Crosswords 21, 22
Ginn 360, Duplicating Masters, Level 6, Sheets 13–15
Key Phonics, Book 3, Pages 43, 44
Learning Phonics 1, Cassette 6
Phonic Bank, Card 42
Phonic Workshop, Cards 53, 54
Phonics – Resource Bank and Teachers' Guide, Sheets N1, N6
Read Write and Spell, Stage 3, Page 30, 31
Reading Quest 5, Pages 8, 9, 36 (O/P)
Sound Sense, Book 8, Pages 43, 44 (O/P)
Sounds and Words, Book 5, Page 12
SRA Schoolhouse, Lime, Cards 17–18
Stile Phonics, Book 12, Pages 2–4
Tree Worksheets 21, 22
Woodpecker, Workbook 9, Places 12–16

Soft 'g' Crossword 20
Ginn 360, Duplicating Masters, Level 8, Sheets 14–16
Level 9, Sheet 7
Key Phonics, Book 3, Page 42, 44
Book 4, Page 13
Learning Phonics 1, Cassette 5
Phonic Bank, Card 43
Phonic Workshop, Cards 48–50
Phonics – Resource Bank and Teachers' Guide, Sheets M1–M5
Read Write and Spell, Stage 3, Pages 34, 36, 39
Stage 4, Page 38
Reading Quest 5, Pages 10, 11 (O/P)
Sound Sense, Book 8, Pages 19, 20 (O/P)

Sounds and Words, Book 5, Page 19
Specific Learning Difficulties Spelling Rules Book 1
SRA Schoolhouse, Lime, Cards 19–20
Stile Phonics, Book 12, Pages 2–4
Tree Workshop 20
Woodpecker, Workbook 9, Pages 12–16

Silent 'b' Active Phonics, Workbook 6
Key Phonics, Book 3, Page 35
Phonic Bank, Card 39
Phonic Links, Book 3, Worksheets 45, 46
Phonics – Resource Bank and Teachers' Guide, Sheet O2, O4
Read Write and Spell, Stage 4, Pages 26, 27

Reading Quest 5, Page 12 (O/P)
Sounds and Words, Book 6, Page 3
Spelling Patterns, Practice Sheet 80
Stile Phonics, Book 12, Page 7

Silent 'c'   Reading Quest 5, Page 18 (O/P)

Silent 'e'   Sounds and Words, Book 5, Page 10

Silent 'g/gh'   Active Phonics, Workbook 6
Ginn 360, Duplicating Masters, Level 9, Sheets 2, 3, 15
Phonic Bank, Card 40
Phonics - Resource Bank and Teachers' Guide, Sheets O1, O4
Read Write and Spell, Stage 4, Pages 26, 27
Reading Quest 5, Page 17 (O/P)
Sound Sense, Book 8, Pages 2, 35, 42 (O/P)

Silent 'k'   Active Phonics, Workbook 6
Ginn 360, Duplicating Masters, Level 7, Sheet 4
Level 9, Sheet 15
Key Phonics, Book 3, Page 24
Phonic Bank, Card 38
Phonic Links, Book 3, Worksheets 45, 46
Phonics – Resource Bank and Teachers' Guide, Sheets O1, O4
Read Write and Spell, Stage 4, Pages 26, 27
Sound Sense, Book 8, Page 42 (O/P)
Sounds and Words, Book 6, Page 2
Stile Phonics, Book 12, Page 7

Silent 'n'   Reading Quest 5, Page 18 (O/P)

Silent 'u'   Reading Quest 5, Page 16 (O/P)
Sounds and Words, Book 6, Page 4

Silent 'w'   Active Phonics, Workbook 6
Ginn 360, Duplicating Masters, Level 9, Sheet 1
Key Phonics, Book 3 , Page 25
Phonic Bank, Card 39
Phonic Links, Book 3, Worksheets 45, 46
Phonics – Resource Bank and Teachers' Guide, Sheet O2
Reading Quest 5, Page 13 (O/P)
Sound Sense, Book 8, Page 42 (O/P)
Sounds and Words, Book 6, Page 1
Stile Phonics, Book 12, Page 8

Silent Letters Revision   Active Phonics, Workbook 6
Phonics Book 9
Phonics – Resource Bank and Teachers' Guide, Sheet O4
Sounds and Words, Book 6, Page 5

Vowel modification by 'r' 'air'   Phonic Bank, Card 44
The Phonics Book (Stanley Thornes)

Sound Sense, Book 8, Page 21
Soundstart Phonic Workshop 2
Sounds and Words, Book 5, Page 5
Spelling Patterns, Practice Sheet 24
SRA Schoolhouse, Yellow, Card 3
Phonic Workshop, Card 37
Woodpecker, Workbook 9, Pages 7, 8

'are' Phonic Bank, Card 44
Phonics – Resource Bank and Teachers' Guide, Sheets K2, K3, K4
The Phonics Book (Stanley Thornes)
Phonic Workshop, Card 38
Sound Sense, Book 8, Page 21
Soundstart Phonic Workshop 2
Sounds and Words, Book 5, Page 5
Spelling Patterns, Practice Sheet 27
SRA Schoolhouse, Yellow, Card 3

'ear' The Phonics Book (Stanley Thornes)
Key Phonics, Book 4, Page 29
Read Write and Spell, Stage 4, Page 50
Soundstart Phonic Workshop 2
Spelling Patterns, Practice Sheet 30
Woodpecker, Workbook 9, Pages 7, 8

'eer' Soundstart Phonic Workshop 2
Woodpecker, Workbook 9, Pages 7, 8

Compound Words Active Phonics, Workbooks 3 and 6
Fuzzbuzz, Letters Book 5, Page 29
Phonic Bank, Card 47
Phonics – Resource Bank and Teachers' Guide, Sheet G2

Polysyllabics Active Phonics, Workbooks 2, 5 and 6
Ginn 360, Duplicating Masters, Level 7, Sheet 1
Level 8, Sheet 7
Phonic Crosspatches
Phonic Bank, Card 48
Sound Sense, Book 5, Page 11
Book 6, Page 5
Book 7, Pages 11, 27
Book 8, Pages 22, 38 (O/P)
Sounds and Words, Book 4, Page 22
Young Shorty Activity Book 1, Pages 19, 20
SRA Schoolhouse, Purple, Cards 1–8
Stile Phonics, Book 11, Page 14
Book 12, Page 1
Timesavers, Phonic Book 6

Contractions Active Phonics, Workbook 6
Fuzzbuzz, Letters Book 5, Page 23
SRA Schoolhouse, Blue, Cards 1–9

Further Materials for the Teaching of Phonics

These materials are not included in the index either because the contents are not suitable for placement in individual phonic categories, or because the material is better used as a self-contained resource.

Beat Dyslexia

(LDA)

A set of four books of copiable worksheets in A4 format, spirally bound. Each book has a corresponding audiotape. Phonic skills covered range from letter sounds to diphthongs, digraphs and letter clusters. The activities provide a multi-sensory approach. Reference sheets and comprehensive teacher's notes are included. Suitable for Key Stage 1 and above. Approximately 100 pages.

The Phonic Reference File

(LDA)

Photocopiable masters in A4 format. Provides a reference resource to support the development and application of a structured approach to teaching phonics. Includes checklists, word lists and diagnostic spelling tests. The materials are designed to identify individual pupil's difficulties, provide appropriate work and monitor progress.

Sound Beginnings

(LDA)

This pack is designed to promote early phonological awareness and comprises 60 A4 photocopiable worksheets, two audio cassettes, 100 cards with full colour illustrations for use with games and a teacher's handbook. Plastic or wooden letters are required for some activities. Suitable for Key Stage 1 or earlier.

Sound Linkage

(Whurr Publishers)

Teacher's reference book providing the basis for a tightly structured phonological awareness programme. Comprehensive lesson plans and teacher's notes on supplementary activities. Approximately 200 pages.

Spotlight on Words

(LDA)

Photocopiable worksheets in A4 format, spirally bound. Designed to supplement spelling and phonic programmes. Activities include word searches and cloze procedure sentences with clear page layouts. Suitable for Key Stages 2 and above; 78 pages.

Stile Dyslexia

(LDA)

A set of eight books in A4 format with full colour illustrations. Designed to support structured spelling and phonic programmes for pupils with specific learning difficulties. Addresses early phonic skills, spelling rules, sequencing and grammar. Suitable for Key Stage 2 and above. Each book contains 166 pages.

Section 13 – Games and Activities

Several publishers produce a variety of games and activities which are valuable aids in the teaching of phonics. Games introduce a welcome 'fun' element to the learning process.

In this section, publishers and items have been arranged alphabetically. Experience has shown that items which have recently disappeared from catalogues may reappear in a revised form a year or so later. Nevertheless, the original version of the game can still be a viable part of a school's stock of phonic resources.

Some games and activities which are integral parts of reading schemes and language programmes have been included in this section because they can also be used in a wider context.

Cambridge University Press
(Shaftesbury Road, Cambridge CB2 2RU Tel: 01223 312393)
Sounds Fun!
This pack of phonic games has been designed to help develop children's knowledge of the sounds that make up words. It concentrates on three early important phonic skills, namely alliteration, rhyming and word building. The pack is based on well-known, traditional card and board games. Items may be used as part of a teaching session to introduce children to sounds or for practising knowledge they already have. The following information is given for each game:

- learning objectives (the phonic skill to be taught or developed);
- level of previous knowledge required;
- equipment needed;
- name of the traditional game on which it is based;
- rules of play;
- other game which could be played with the same equipment;
- a checklist of components;
- notes on ways in which games may be adapted for different ability levels.

The games included are:
    Sounds Around – understanding alliteration;
    Match the Sound – recognising sounds: s, t, p, b, m, d, w, g, f, r, j, n;
    Rhyme Time – understanding rhyming;
    Rhyming Snap, Rhyming Pairs, Rhyming Families – recognising words which belong to the same rhyming family;
    Rhyming Lotto – rhyming families;
    Rhyming Dominoes – matching words that rhyme;
    Make a Word and *Find the Hidden Words* – word building;
    Wordmaking Dominoes – word building.

Drake Educational Associates
(St Fagan's Road, Fairwater, Cardiff CF5 3AE Tel: 01222 560333)
Action Phonics
Presented as 14 self-contained modules, this series for the Language Master is carefully structured to enable the pupil to grasp each individual phonic skill at his or her own pace. The skills covered include initial consonants, final consonants, vowels, consonant vowel blends, initial consonant blends, consonant digraphs, vowel digraphs and silent consonants.
Sound Reading
Three sets of cards designed to give practice in phonic skills. Each set contains 20 reading cards

with 12 phonic exercises on each card: 1 – initial and final consonants; 2 – consonant vowel blends; 3 – initial and final consonant blends and digraphs.

Word Blending

Using Language Master cards, this kit is intended to reinforce the blending of individual letter sounds into words. The programme covers all the initial consonant and short vowel blends.

Word Study

This programme for the Language Master covers 113 different areas of phonic difficulty. A combination of sight and sound enables pupils to look at a letter or group of letters printed on a card while, at the same time, listening to the sounds associated with them. The kit contains 113 Language Master cards, four sets of word/picture cards, a set of word dominoes, four picture masks and other items.

James Galt and Company Ltd

(Brookfield Road, Cheadle, Cheshire SK8 2PN Tel: 0161 428 8511)

Alpha Tiles

This set comprises 26 lower case plastic letter tiles and 78 picture tiles. Can be used for letter name and sound recognition and word building.

Letter Match

Letters of the alphabet are illustrated on thick cardboard tiles which have been cut into three parts. Pieces fit together to make complete letter cards. Suitable for 3–6 year-olds.

Picture-Word Dominoes

All the words used are phonically regular with high-frequency initial consonants. Provides practice for children who are just beginning to build words. Comprises two colour-coded sets of 20 cards.

Sound Lotto

A lotto game to encourage early word recognition and spelling. Includes four game boards.

Word Building Blends

An effective game for learning 24 initial and final consonant blends.

Initial blends: bl, fl, gl, br, dr, gr, tr, sn, sp, st, sw.

Final blends and digraphs: -ch, -ck, -it, -mp, -ng, -nk, -ns, -sh, -st, -th.

Word Middles

Deals with C-V-C words. Players find the correct medial vowel to complete the spelling of a word which related to a particular picture. Includes four game boards.

GAMZ

(25 Albert Park Road, Malvern, Worcestershire WR14 1HW Tel: 01684 562158)

SWAP Card Games

Fourteen card games which have been developed by SpLD tutors and used successfully through the age range 6–16. Fifty cards in each pack and a set of simple rules:

Game 1   – a, e, i, o, u;
Game 2   – ch, sh, th;
Game 3   – -ff, -ll, -ss, -zz, -ck;
Game 4   – a-e, e-e, i-e, o-e, u-e;
Game 5   – ai, ay, ee, ea, oa;
Game 6   – er, ir, ur, ear;
Game 7   – air, are, ear, eir, ere;
Game 8   – or, aw, au, oor, our;
Game 9   – wa, wor, war, -ward;
Game 10 – silent letters t, h, b, k, w;
Game 11 – -y, -uy, -ie, i-e, igh;

Game 12 – oo, ew, ue, ui, ou;

Game 13 – -er, -ar, -or, -our;

Game 14 – -tion, -cian, -ssion, -sion, -shion.

H.E.L.P Educational Games

(29 Churchill Close, Didcot, Oxfordshire OX11 7BX Tel: 01235 817241)

Odd Bods – A jigsaw game which teaches the first 24 most used words (suitable for children 4–7+ years).

Chase – key word recognition (6–11).

Blend-It – building three letter word (5–9).

Blend-It Again – blend at the end of the word and a picture clue for the initial sound (5–9).

Match and Rhyme Dominoes – initial and final consonant blends (6–11).

Glug – initial consonant blends (6–11).

Plunder – magic 'e' words (7–11).

Remember, Remember – magic 'e'.

Scoop! – vowel digraphs: ea, ai, ee, ou, oa, ui, oi, au (7+).

Black Hole – C-V-C blending (9–13).

Secret Sid – silent letters in words (9+).

Penalty – vowel digraphs (8–13).

Bugs – three-in-one game: b, d, p confusion; C-V-C blends; final consonant blends (7–11).

Link-It – final consonant blends: -nd, -nk, -mp, -nt, -ck (7–11).

Splash – syllables (9+).

Pounce – soft 'c' and 'g' words (9+).

Swat – words with 'w' rules (9+).

Jolly Learning Ltd

(Clare Hall, Chapel Lane, Chigwell, Essex IG7 6JJ Tel: 0181 500 1696)

Finger Phonic Books

Seven books, made from stiff cardboard, cover the 40+ sounds of English. Grooved letter shapes on each page guide the pupils to trace the correct formation of letters. There are actions for each sound and the series complements *The Phonic Handbook* by Sue Lloyd (from the same publisher). A *Phonic Frieze* is available to accompany each book:

Book/Frieze 1 – s, a, t, i, p, n;

Book/Frieze 2 – c, k, e, h, r, m, d;

Book/Frieze 3 – g, o, u, 1, f, b;

Book/Frieze 4 – ai, j, oa, ie, ee, or;

Book/Frieze 5 – z, w, ng, v, short 'oo', long 'oo';

Book/Frieze 6 – y, x, ch, sh, voiced 'th', unvoiced 'th';

Book/Frieze 7 – qu, ou, oi, ue, er, ar.

Jiglets

For children aged 3–6, these flexible magnetic jigsaw puzzles are ideal for fridge doors, upturned metal tea trays or metal chalkboards. They provide a simple introduction to spelling:

Schools Animal Pack – dog, cat, pig, hen;

Schools Vehicle Pack – car, van, bus, boat.

Letter Sounds

Devised by Betty Root, this series of matching games is intended for 4–8 year-olds:

Donkey   – story book and matching sounds;

Rook   – story book and initial sounds;

Rabbit   – story book and sounds quiz game;

Goat   – story book and rhyming words;

Toad   – story book and word building game;
    Cocky Cockerel – story book and double sounds (tr, pl etc.)

Piklets

A set of eight boards, each with six or seven illustrations. Cards in the accompanying wallet have an initial letter sound on one side and a word on the other. Children (3–6) match the cards to the illustrations.

Stencilets

Durable, washable plastic stencils, each with a picture and a word. The Stencilets fold over and clip shut, so that a sheet of A5 paper can be held in place. The illustration inside provides an example for completing the drawing: dog, van, man, hut, hat, cat, bus, pig.

Learning Development Aids (LDA)

(Duke Street, Wisbech, Cambridgeshire PE13 2AE Tel: 01223 365445)

Blend Dominoes

A set of 108 dominoes to give children practice in phonic blends.

Dealing with Vowels

A pack of 64 cards which uses familiar games such as Happy Families, Snap and Pelmanism to reinforce vowel digraphs:

    Set 1 – ay, ou, ee, ei, oo, aw, y;
    Set 2 – ai, oa, ow, ea, oy, oo, ew, ey.

Funkey Blends

Using traditional card games that children know and enjoy (such as Rummy, Memory, Fish and Snap), each game focuses on one particular aspect of phonics. Each set contains 55 cards and can be used for several different games. Useful for the 6–12 age group:

Matching and Grouping	– alphabet sounds and categorisation;
Dreadful Dragons	– consonant blends;
Double Trouble	– easy digraphs and vowel digraphs such as sh, ch, th, wh;
Double Trouble 2	– more difficult vowel digraphs including aw, au;
Magic 'e'	– long vowels with final 'e' sound;
Tricky Endings	– recognition and spelling of endings including: -augh; -tion; -ight; -age; -ly; -tain; -sion; -tine; -ic; -ful; -ould; -sion.

I-Spy

Developed from the traditional game, this set contains four double-sided game cards plus a spinner offering a choice of 24 letters. It is helpful in reinforcing children's recognition of initial letters. There is also a UNICEF version of this game.

Minimal Pairs Lotto/Minimal Match

This consists of four simple lotto games which help pupils to discriminate between similar-looking and sounding words and to encourage them to link the correct sound with the correct meaning. The games are graded.

Paper Chains – Phonics

A set of 200 cards, comprising 25 games, each of eight cards. Easily learned and completely self-checking, *Paper Chains* is helpful for struggling readers of all ages. The progression begins with consonant-vowel-consonant (C-V-C) words and moves to C-V-CC words.

Sound Beginnings

This pack draws on methods and activities used in phonological awareness studies in order to enable practitioners to identify children's difficulties. It then enables them to make immediate and effective provision at an early stage.

    The package also includes a teacher's handbook; 60 photocopiable activity sheets; 100 cards to use for the games and activities; and two audiotapes.

The LDA Wordbuilding Box

There are 116 wooden letters in Rosemary Sassoon's 'Primary font', sufficient for pupils to make words and build sentences. Also recommended for use with *Sound Beginnings*, described above.

Oxford University Press

(Walton Street, Oxford OX2 6DP Tel: 01865 56767)

Rhyme and Analogy

This range of resources is aimed at developing children's phonological awareness. It has been devised to teach them the alphabet and letter sounds, and to develop their ability to hear and identify rhymes. As an integral part of *Oxford Reading Tree*, it can be introduced from Stage 1 onwards. Its components are such that it could easily be integrated with other reading schemes or phonic programmes.

In recent years, it has been increasingly recognised that an awareness of rhyming and alliteration is important for children to become good readers. The research and linguistic background is clearly explained in the *Teacher's Guide*, together with its practical application to the reading of young children.

Components include:

Story Rhymes – central to the programme, Packs A and B are built around a graded structure of rhyming words, with four clue rhymes being included in each story;

Story Rhyme Big Books – *Story Rhymes* in large format;

Story Rhyme and *Alphabet Photocopy Masters*;

Alphabet Frieze;

Tabletop Alphabet Mats – similar to the Frieze;

Card Games – more than 50 games can be played with the four card sets;

Story Rhyme Tapes – 12 *Story Rhymes* recorded on six cassettes.

Philip and Tacey

(North Way, Andover, Hampshire SP10 5BA Tel: 01264 332171)

Alphabet Dominoes

A set of 27 double-sided, varnished domino cards designed to aid letter recognition and initial letter sounds. The dominoes are double sided, thus providing two different activities. One side involves picture-letter matching, the other helps pupils to match upper and lower case letters. Both activities are self-correcting.

Alphabet Floor Puzzle

Made of 28 thick cardboard pieces, this puzzle helps children to learn the alphabet.

Approach Picture and Word-Building Cards

A three-part matching activity which provides practice in building simple three-letter words. There are five boxes, each of which contains six inset boards. Each board has a picture, underneath which is a word and a slot for inserting matched letters.

Busy Bee Word Games

Three games designed to reinforce letter blend and encourage word building. Three different sets of 60 hexagonal cards, each showing a blend or digraph, are combined in play on a colourful 'beehive' base board to produce a variety of words.

Hexablanks are available for creating additional or replacement cards according to individual needs.

Clearview Picture Crossword Puzzles

A set of graded puzzles presented on varnished A4 cards with clues in the form of easily identifiable illustrations:

Set 1: Phonic – deals with short vowels (a, e, i, o, u); long vowels (a–e, ai, ea, ee, o–e, i–e); medial vowels (oo and oa); and the vowel digraph 'ow'.

Consonantal Blend Strips

This game for two to four players provides practice and reinforcement of 14 of the most common letter blends and consonantal digraphs.

Each blend strip features an initial blend or digraph. Pupils can *either* match four clearly illustrated picture cards which represent that blend *or* four corresponding word cards. In addition, the word and picture cards can be used as a separate matching activity.

Consonant-Vowel Blend Matching Cards

A set of self-correcting matching cards. The word splits between the vowel and the final consonant or digraph in order to help pupils with this important aspect of phonic discrimination.

Cromwell Word-Making Activities

Two sets of sorting and matching activities using plastic trays and colour-coded cards:

> *Set 1 — Blend and Digraph Word-Making Activities*
> For sorting and matching groups of words containing the same initial blend or digraph.
>
> *Set 2 — Word-Making From Half-Way Words*
> Pupils build their own words from a range of half-cards. Each bears either an initial blend or digraph, or a word ending.

The Haunted House: A Co-operative Game

In this board game, up to four players have a set of clearly illustrated picture cards representing an initial consonant. When someone gets trapped in the haunted house, fellow players have to combine their cards to free him or her.

Initial Consonant Blends with Phonic Endings

The set includes 21 initial consonant blends and ch, sh, wh, with 15 phonic endings to produce 24 specific words. A card containing the word and ending only is matched with a separate card bearing the initial blend.

Initial Consonantal Digraph Word Building Games

Two simple games designed to reinforce initial letter blends and consonantal digraphs. Each recessed card is completed with two components, one digraph and one phoneme, from a central pool.

Initial Digraph Activity Cards

Similar in presentation to the *Phonic Alphabet Activity Cards*, this set of 28 laminated cards introduces a range of digraphs and letter blends including: br, bl, cl, ch, dr, fl, gr, gl, kn, ph, p1, pr, sc, sk, sl, sw, sm, sh, sn, st, sp, th, tr, tw, wh, wr.

Make-a-Word Spelling Game

A set of two games which give practice in word recognition and word making. Players build words by drawing letters from a central pool and matching them to the uncovered letters on their base cards.

New Colet Alphabet Pictures and Sounds Matching Cards

Twenty-eight pairs of cards for matching pictures and initial letter sounds, including the alternative styles for 'a' and 'g'.

New Chelsea Pictorial Alphabet

A colourfully illustrated visual aid which is designed to teach the alphabet and letter sounds.

Noah's Ark Alphabet

Interlocking cardboard pieces go to make up a puzzle in which each letter is illustrated with the picture of an animal or bird. Suitable for floor play.

Phonic Alphabet Activity Cards

A set of 24 (x, y and z are on one card) laminated cards provides an introduction to initial letter sounds and helps pupils to build up a basic vocabulary. The cut-out of the main picture allows for extension activities. There is a letter panel on the reverse of each card to aid writing practice.

Picture and Sound Alphabet Cellograph Display Cards

A set of wall display cards, each featuring a colourful illustration, a key letter and a sample word. Each card has a blank panel below, in which further examples of words may be written.

Use of a special pencil is advisable, in order that the laminated surface can be wiped clean.

Real Things Food and Drink: Alphabet Matching Cards

A set of 26 double-sided, laminated, matching cards using initial letter sounds and photographs of food and drink. Cards are cut in a simple and distinctive way, thus ensuring that young children can match the two parts and join them easily. The activity is self-correcting.

Sort and Sound Vowel Digraph Cards

Four sets, each containing nine laminated cards. The cards are cut into three sections. The middle strip of each puzzle introduces the following vowel sounds: ee, ea, oi, ie, oo (as in 'moon') and oo (as in 'book').

Sort and Sound Word-Making Cards

Six sets, each containing nine laminated cards. As above, the cards are cut into three sections. When the puzzles are assembled, they make three or four letter words, focusing on single sounds and initial and final consonant digraphs.

Spin-and-Spell Spelling Game

Suitable for up to four players. Pupils match letters to the 'spinner' and use them to build words on their word cards. Comprises 20 word cards, 60 letters and a spinner printed with 12 letters.

Vowel Sound Snap Games

These simple vowel snap games introduce the five vowels. Each card features either a word and an illustration, or simply a word. The game is played as in traditional Snap, except that a word card can also be matched with a picture card. There is a separate box of cards for each vowel, plus a sixth assorted box.

Vowel and Digraph Completion Slides

Words are completed by inserting a missing vowel or digraph. Picture cards are slotted into a retaining channel. The corresponding words are completed by selecting a transparent plastic rectangle on which is printed a single or double letter phoneme. This is then slid into the channel and moved along until the appropriate word is completed.

Vowel Sounds Sorting Box

There are 24 laminated cards and a sorting box. The activity is designed to reinforce vowel recognition. Previously known as *Sussex Vowel Sorting and Word Cards*.

Taskmaster

(Morris Road, Leicester LE2 6BR Tel: 0116 270 4286)

Alphabet Matching Puzzles

Comprises 26 two-piece puzzles. Upper and lower case letters are matched to illustrations of animals and familiar objects.

Consonant Blends and Digraph Puzzles

A set of 30 puzzles designed to help pupils with basic blends and digraphs.

Linkaword

A set of 24 plastic triangles which can be linked together to form random shapes or one large hexagon. In doing so, consonantal blends and digraphs are linked with word endings to make words.

Linkaword Endings

Similar to one described previously, this game concentrates on common word endings:

    Set 1 – -le, -ght, -ing, -ong;

    Set 2 – -y, -ace, -in, -im, -op, -ack, -ick, -ar.

Silent Consonants Puzzles

A set of 30 puzzle cards help pupils to recognise the silent consonant in each word by matching the picture/word side of the puzzle with the silent letter on the other puzzle piece.

Sounds and Syllables

A set of three card games:

1. *Same Sound Snap and Rummy* – long a, e, i, o digraphs.
    Pupils match digraphs which look different but sound the same (*homophones*, eg made paid).
2. *Rhyming Snap* – extends digraph matching to include common irregular words.
3. *Syllable Snap and Rummy* – words are matched by the number of syllables.

Vowels and Blends

Three simple card games using short vowel sounds:

1. *Short Vowel Sound Snap and Rummy* – short vowel sounds.
2. *First Blends Snap 1* – initial consonantal blends: bl, cl, cr, dr, fr, gr, pl, pr.
3. *First Blends Snap 2* – initial blends: tr, th, sh, ch, sm, st.

Word Hexagons

Three word completion games featuring 'Naming Words' (orange), 'Describing Words' (red) and 'Action Words' (green), by the correct linking of word beginnings with word endings, the 24 plastic triangles in each set will form a hexagon with a coloured border.

Wordspell

Three sets of word games, each for four players. Each game has four different word boards and 'cards' made of plastic:

Sets 1 and 2 – The object of both games is for players to place digraph cards on the board against appropriate endings in order to form correct words and to score points. *Set 1* uses simple familiar vocabulary. *Set 2* includes all the common double vowel combinations.

Set 3 – Players match the endings printed on the cards with initial consonant blends and digraphs on the boards.

Section 14 – Computer Software

Software Agents
AVP, Unit 3, School Hill Centre, Chepstow, Gwent NP6 5PH Tel: 01291 625 439.

Children's Computing, Unit D, 3A Telford Road, Bicester, Oxfordshire OX6 0TZ Tel: 01869 324 324.

Dyslexia Educational Resources, Broadway Studios, 28 Tooting High Street, London SW17 0RG Tel: 0181 672 4465.

Rickitt Educational Media, Great Western House, Langport, Somerset TA10 9YU Tel: 01458 253 636.

SEMERC, 1 Broadbent Road, Watersheddings, Oldham OL1 4LB Tel: 0161 627 4469.

Shareware Addresses
Brown Bag Software, 3a Queen Street, Seaton, Devon EX12 2NY.

PC Shareware Magazine, L'Avenir Corporation, Westbrook Building, Thornton Road, Bradford BD1 2DX.

SMS Shareware, 19 Carshalton Road, Camberley, Surrey GU15 4AQ Tel: 01276 681 864.

Testware, 46 The Avenue, Harrogate, North Yorkshire HG1 4QD Tel: 01423 886 415.

Vasstec, 1485 Dunbarton Road, Glasgow G14 9XL.

Software Houses
Ablac Computec Ltd, South Devon House, Newton Abbott, Devon TQ12 2BP Tel: 01626 332 233.

ACCESS CENTRES, National Federation of ACCESS Centres, Hereward College of Further Education, Bramston Crescent, Tile Hill Lane, Coventry CV4 9SW Tel: 01203 461 231.

ACE Centre, Waynflete Road, Headington, Oxford OX3 8DD Tel: 01865 63508.

Apt Projects, PO Box 1066, Belton, South Yorkshire DN8 1QX Tel: 01427 875 103.

Borland, Tracline Ltd, Bennet House, 1 High Street, Edgeware, HA8 7TH Tel: 0181 951 4712.

Broderbund, Softline Distribution Ltd, 123 Westmead Road, Sutton, Surrey SM1 4JH Tel: 0181 642 2255.

Camsoft, 10 Wheatfield Close, Maidenhead, Berkshire SL6 3PS Tel: 01628 825 206.

CENPAC, Charlton Park School, Charlton Park Road, London SE7 8HX Tel: 0181 316 7589.

Chalksoft, 37 Willowslea Road, Worcester WR3 7PQ Tel: 01905 55192.

Colton, 8 Signet Court, Swann's Road, Cambridge CB4 8LA Tel: 01223 311 881.

Computer Campus, 4 Romney Drive, Bromley, Kent BR1 2TE Tel: 0181 464 1330.

Computibility Centre, PO Box 94, Warwick CV34 5WS Tel: 0800 269 545.

Crick Computing, 123 The Drive, Northampton NN1 4SW Tel: 01604 713 686.

Daco Software, 463 Warwick Road, Tysley, Birmingham Tel: 0121 706 8933.

Daisy Multimedia, Vincent Court, Fishes Green Road, Stevenage, Hertfordshire SG1 2PT
Tel: 01438 745 300.

Drake Educational Associates, St Fagans Road, Fairwater, Cardiff CF5 3AE Tel: 01222 560 333.

Egon Publishers Ltd, Royston Road, Baldock, Hertfordshire SG7 6NW Tel: 01462 894 498.

EMU, Sandwell Training and Development Centre, Popes Lane, Oldbury, Warley B69 4PJ
Tel: 0121 569 4400.

E.S.M., Ambergate House, East Road, Cambridge CB1 1DB.

Europress Software, Europa House, Adlington Park, Adlington, Macclesfield SK10 4NP
Tel: 01625 895 333.

Folio Publications, Tediman Software, PO Box 23, Southampton, Hampshire SO9 7BD.

4Mation, 14 Castle Park Road, Barnstaple, Devon EX23 8PA Tel: 01271 25353.

Fisher Marriot, 3 Grove Road, Ansty, Coventry CV7 9JD Tel: 01203 616 235.

Flexible Software, PO Box 100, Abingdon, Oxfordshire OX13 6PQ Tel: 01865 391 148.

H.S. Software, Hendrefoilan Avenue, Sketty, Swansea, Glamorgan SA2 7NB Tel: 01792 204 519.

Iansyst, The White House, 72 Fen Road, Cambridge CB4 1UN Tel: 01223 420 273.

I.E.C., 77 Orton Lane, Wombourne, Staffordshire WV5 9AP Tel: 01902 892 599.

Kosmos, 1 Pilgrims Close, Harlington, Dunstable, Bedfordshire LU5 6LX Tel: 01525 873 942.

Kudliuan Soft, 8 Barrows Road, Kenilworth, Warwickshire CV8 1EH Tel: 01926 251 147.

Lander, 74 Victorian Crescent Road, Glasgow G12 9JN Tel: 0141 357 1659.

Literacy Development Company, 8 Thorndales, Brentwood, Essex CM14 5DE
Tel: 01277 229 093.

Lotus Developments, Lotus Park, Staines, Middlesex TW18 3AG Tel: 01784 445 925.

Lucid Systems, 26 Tunis Street, Sculcoates Lane, Hull HU5 1EZ Tel: 01482 465 589.

MarkChrisSoft, 6 Howard House, Mary Hare Grammar School, Newbury, Berkshire RG16 9BQ.

Microsoft, Wharfdale Road, Winnersh Triangle, Wokingham, Berkshire RG11 5TP.

NCET, Milburn Hill Road, Science Park, Coventry CV4 7JJ Tel: 01203 416 994.

NORICC, Resources Centre, Coach Lane Campus, Northern Coach Lane, Newcastle Upon Tyne NE7 7XA Tel: 0191 270 0424.

Sage Business Software, Sage House, Benton Park Road, Newcastle Upon Tyne NE7 7LZ Tel: 0191 201 0600.

Sherston Software, Angel House, Sherston, Malmesbury, Wiltshire SN16 0LH Tel: 01666 840 433.

SITSS, Shropshire IT Support Services, Bourne House, Radbrook Centre, Shrewsbury SY3 9BJ Tel: 01743 246 043.

SPA, PO Box 59, Tewkesbury, GL20 6AB Tel: 01684 833 700.

Starnet Ltd, Dept. RX1, PO Box 21, Malvern, Worcestershire WR14 2DX.

Storm Software, Coachman's Quarters, Digby Road, Sherbourne, Dorset DT9 3NN Tel: 01935 817 699.

Tag Developments Ltd, 19 High Street, Gravesend DA11 0BA Tel: 01474 357 350.

Technomatic, Techno House, 468 Church Lane, London NW9 8UF Tel: 0181 205 9558.

White Space Ltd, 41 Mall Road, London W6 9DG Tel: 0181 748 5927.

Widget, 1 The Ryde, Hatfield, Hertfordshire Tel: 0707 264 780.

WordPerfect, Weybridge Business Park, Addlestone Road, Addlestone, Surrey KT15 2UU Tel: 01932 850 505.

Software Publishers/Suppliers (in alphabetical order)

Chalksoft	Letters and Pictures
Daco	Readwell
Drake Educational Associates	*Visual Discrimination Series* Objects-Letters-Shapes Letters Reversals and Inversions
	Visual Memory Series Objects-Letters-Shapes Letters Reversals and Inversions
	Language Centre Series Initial Consonants Short Vowels Compound Words Jumbled Words Initial Consonant Blends Silent Letters Final Consonant Blends

EMU	Firs Phonics
ESM	An Eye For Spelling
	Hands on Spelling
H. S. Software	*Read Right Away Reading Pack 1*
	Splashdown
	Firefight
	Read Right Away Reading Pack 2
	Pyramids
	Sploosh
	Read Right Away Reading Pack 3
	Magic e (b)
	Break In
Folio Publications	Word Attack Strategies
SEMERC	*Part of My World Suite*
	Alphabet
	Early Phonics
	My Speech
	Stand Alone Software
	Claude and Maud
	Letters and Numbers
	Speakeasy
	Play on Words Suite (Can be purchased individually)
	ABC
	Crab
	n blends
	s and t blends
	Shoot
Sherston Software	Animated Alphabet
	Consonant Blends
	Magic e (c)
	Short Vowel Sounds
	Vowel Digraphs (a)
Starnet Ltd	Let's Learn Phonics
Widget	From Pictures to Words
Xavier	Alpha Sound
	Part of Arcspell 1 BBC Suite (Can be purchased individually)
	Word Maze

Part of Hispell 2 BBC Suite (Can be purchased separately)
Fortress
Magic e (a)
Matcher
Splitter
Vowel Digraphs (b)

Part of Hispell 3 BBC Suite (Can be purchased separately)
Bagatelle
Driver
Suffixing

Arcspell 1 Suite (Acorn single disc)
Bagatelle
Magic e (a)
Word Maze

Arcspell 2 Suite (Acorn single disc)
Splitter
Suffixing
Vowel Digraphs (b)

Other Software from Xavier
Beedee
Chooser
Magic e (b)
Soapbox
Sounds & Rhymes
Yog and the Nippet

Phonic skills covered by the software programs in the index

	ABC	Alphabet	Alpha Sound	An Eye for Spelling	Animated Alphabet	Arcspell 1	Arcspell 2	Bagatelle	Beedee	Break In	Chooser
Sound Blaster requ'd											
PC		●									
Acorn	●	●	●	●		●	●				●
BBC					●			●	●		
Speech Output			●								●
Compound Words							●				
Patterns				●							
b/d Confusion									●		
Soft c/g										●	
Magic e						●					
Modified by r											
Vowel Digraphs						●	●	●			
Final Blends											
ch, ph, sh, th, wh											
Initial Blends											
c-v-c						●					●
Initial Letters	●	●			●						
Rhyming											

95

Phonic skills covered by the software programs in the index

	Claude and Maude	Compound Words	Consonant Blends	Crab	Driver	Early Phonics		Ervaders	Final Consonant Blends	Firefight	Firs Phonics
Sound Blaster requ'd											
PC						●					
Acorn	●			●		●		●		●	
BBC		●	●		●			●	●	●	●
Speech Output	●			●							
Compound Words		●									
Patterns											
b/d Confusion											
Soft c/g					●						●
Magic e											●
Modified by r								●			●
Vowel Digraphs											●
Final Blends									●	●	●
ch, ph, sh, th, wh											●
Initial Blends				●	●					●	●
c-v-c											●
Initial Letters	●					●					
Rhyming											

96

Phonic skills covered by the software programs in the index

	Fortress	From Pictures To Words	Initial Consonants	Initial Consonant Blends	Jumbled Words	Letters	Letters and Patterns	Letters and Numbers	Letter Recognition	Let's Learn Phonics	Magic e (a)
Sound Blaster requ'd											
PC								●			
Acorn	●							●			
BBC		●	●	●	●	●	●		●	●	●
Speech Output											
Compound Words											
Patterns											
b/d Confusion											
Soft c/g											●
Magic e										●	●
Modified by r	●									●	
Vowel Digraphs										●	
Final Blends										●	
ch, ph, sh, th, wh										●	
Initial Blends				●						●	
c-v-c							●			●	
Initial Letters		●	●			●	●	●	●	●	
Rhyming											

Phonic skills covered by the software programs in the index

	Magic e (b)	Magic e (c)	Matcher	My Speech	n blends	Objects Letters Shapes	Pyramids	Read Right Away 1	Read Right Away 2	Read Right Away 3	Readwell
Sound Blaster requ'd											
PC							●				
Acorn	●			●	●		●				
BBC		●	●			●	●	●	●	●	●
Speech Output	●			●	●						
Compound Words											
Patterns											
b/d Confusion											
Soft c/g										●	
Magic e	●	●								●	●
Modified by r											●
Vowel Digraphs									●		●
Final Blends											●
ch, ph, sh, th, wh							●		●		●
Initial Blends					●		●				●
c-v-c							●				●
Initial Letters			●	●		●	●				
Rhyming			●								

Phonic skills covered by the software programs in the index

	Reversals / Inversions	s and t blends	Shoot	Short Vowels	Short Vowel Sounds	Silent Letters	Soapbox	Sounds and Rhymes	Speakeasy	Splashdown	Sploosh
Sound Blaster requ'd											
PC										●	●
Acorn		●	●				●	●	●	●	
BBC	●			●	●	●				●	
Speech Output		●	●				●	●	●		
Compound Words							●				
Patterns											
b / d Confusion	●										
Soft c / g											
Magic e									●		
Modified by r											
Vowel Digraphs			●								●
Final Blends											
ch, ph, sh, th, wh			●								
Initial Blends		●									
c-v-c				●	●			●	●	●	
Initial Letters											
Rhyming							●	●			

Phonic skills covered by the software programs in the index

	Vowel Digraphs (a)	Vowel Digraphs (b)	Vowel Digraphs (c)	Word Attack Strategies	Word Maze	Word Shark 2	Words on Spelling	Yog & The Nippet		
Sound Blaster requ'd						●				
PC						●				
Acorn			●							
BBC	●	●		●	●		●	●		
Speech Output						●				
Compound Words						●				
Patterns							●			
b/d Confusion										
Soft c/g				●						
Magic e				●		●				
Modified by r				●						
Vowel Digraphs	●	●	●	●		●				
Final Blends				●						
ch, ph, sh, th, wh				●						
Initial Blends				●						
c-v-c					●					
Initial Letters								●		
Rhyming								●		

Section 15 – Phonic Word Lists

These are lists of words which relate to the main phonic conventions. Every effort has been made to grade the lists so that the most difficult phonic element in the word is the one receiving attention. The lists are provided as a resource for teachers who need ready access to a series of words for teaching a particular skill.

With the ever-growing use of computers with desk top publishing software, it is relatively simple to produce high-quality word cards or worksheets if a list of suitable words is readily available.

When selecting words it is helpful to pay due regard to the life experience of the child so that words chosen are within the child's experience and spoken vocabulary. This is particularly important with either young children or those from ethnic minority groups.

Short Vowel a

bad	bat
Dad	cat
had	fat
mad	hat
pad	sat
sad	mat
ham	rat
jam	can
Pam	bag
Sam	rag
can	
fan	
man	
Nan	
pan	
ran	
cap	
tap	
map	
at	

Short Vowel e

jet	hen
let	ten
net	men
pet	get
set	red
wet	pen
yet	den
beg	leg
let	Ben
Meg	
peg	
yes	
bet	
met	
bed	
fed	
led	
Ned	
Ted	
wed	

Short Vowel i

did	lit
hid	pit
lid	sit
big	wit
dig	is
fig	bid
jig	Jim
pig	hip
wig	his
bin	bib
din	pip
fin	rib
pin	mix
sin	fix
tin	dip
win	nip
it	kid
bit	zip
fit	him
hit	

Short Vowel o

hop	pot
lop	on
mop	Ron
pop	box
top	fox
bog	cod
dog	rod
fog	nod
log	dot
got	top
hot	hop
lot	sob
rot	rob
tot	god
cot	Tom
jot	Don
not	

Short Vowel u

up	sun
cup	us
pup	bus
but	bug
cut	hug
gut	mug
hut	jug
jut	rug
nut	dug
Mum	put
hum	rub
rum	cub
sum	tub
bun	bud
fun	
gun	
run	

Consonant Digraph ch

chap	bunch
chat	munch
chin	bench
chip	pinch
chit	hunch
chop	winch
chub	
chug	
chum	
champ	
chimp	
rich	
much	
such	
lunch	
punch	

Consonant Digraph sh

sham	dash
shed	dish
shin	fish
ship	gash
shod	gosh
shop	gush
shot	hash
shun	hush
shut	lash
shift	lush
shunt	mash
ash	mesh
bash	sash
bosh	rash
cash	posh
cosh	mush

Consonant Digraph th

than
that
them
then
this
thus
with
bath
moth
pith
thin
thud
thug

Final Consonant Digraph ck

jack	muck	rick	tick	dock
Jock	neck	rock	tuck	duck
kick	nick	ruck	wick	hack
lack	pack	sack	back	hock
lick	peck	sick	beck	
lock	pick	sock	buck	
luck	pock	suck	cock	
mock	rack	tack	deck	

Final Consonant Blends

pant	best	hump	lend	gong
bent	bust	jump	mend	song
dent	cast	gasp	band	sung
went	cost	rasp	helm	lung
hunt	dust	held	gulp	bank
punt	fast	weld	bump	junk
mask	fist	self	camp	rung
task	gust	gulf	damp	pump
desk	jest	silk	lamp	sunk
risk	tusk	bulk	limp	sink
dusk	next	sulk	lump	rink
husk	text	help	ramp	rank
rent	kept	belt	sump	sank
sent	wept	felt	send	tank
tent	soft	melt	fund	link
daft	lift	gilt	bond	mink
gift	tuft	kilt	fond	pink
loft	left	silt	pond	honk
raft	romp	hand	rang	bunk
cask	vent	land	sang	sunk
tusk	golf	sand	ring	wind
next	film	end	sing	wink
text	bump	bend	long	

Initial Consonant Blends

bl	**dr**	grid	**sc**	stud
blab	drab	grim	scab	stun
bled	drag	grin	scan	
blob	dram	grip	scat	**sw**
blot	drat	grit	scot	swag
black	dreg	grog	scud	swam
block	drip	grub	scum	swig
blush	drop	grist		swim
blast	drug			swop
blest	drum		**sk**	swum
		pl	skid	swing
		plan	skin	swish
br	**fl**	plod	skip	
brag	flab	plop	skit	
bran	flag	plot		**tr**
brat	flan	plug		tram
brig	flap	plum	**sm**	trap
brim	flat	plus	smog	trek
brick	flax	pluck	smug	trim
brock	fled	plush	smut	trip
bring	flex		smack	trod
brash	flip		smock	track
brush	flit	**pr**	smash	trick
broth	flog	pram		truck
	flop	prig		trash
	flux	prim	**sn**	trust
cl	fleck	prod	snag	troth
clad	flick	prop	snap	
clam	flock		snip	
clan	fling		snob	**tw**
clap	flash	**sl**	snub	twig
clef	flesh	slab	snack	twin
clip	flush	slag	snick	twit
clod		slam		
clog		slap		
clot	**fr**	slat	**sp**	
club	fret	sled	span	
click	frit	slid	spat	
clock	frog	slim	sped	
cling	from	slip	spin	
clamp	frock	slit	spit	
cluck	frost	slob	spot	
clash	froth	slog	spud	
		slop	spun	
		slot	speck	
cr	**gl**	slub	spick	
crab	glad	slug		
crag	glen	slum		
cram	glug	slut	**st**	
crib	glum	slack	stab	
crop	glut	slick	stag	
crack		sling	stem	
crash		slash	sten	
crush	**gr**	slosh	step	
crest	grab	slush	stop	
crust	gran		stub	

r words with initial digraphs and final blends

	chunk	shunt	stink	stunk
	shaft	stamp	stint	theft
	shank	stand	stomp	think
chink	shelf	stank	stump	thump
chump	shift	stilts	stunt	thank

Regular words with initial and final blends

bland	clink	drift	grasp	skunk	swept
blank	clomp	drink	grunt	slant	swift
blend	clonk	drunk	plank	slept	tramp
blink	clump	dwelt	plant	slink	trend
blond	clunk	flank	plonk	slump	trump
blunt	craft	flint	plump	slunk	trunk
brand	cramp	frank	prank	smelt	
brink	crank	frisk	plinth	smash	
brisk	crept	frump	print	spank	
brunt	crimp	gland	scalp	spelt	
clamp	crisp	glint	scamp	spend	
clank	croft	graft	scant	spent	
clasp	draft	grand	skimp	split	
cleft	drank	grant	skulk	swank	

Magic e with a

cake	gate	plate
make	hate	skate
rake	late	slate
lake	mate	slave
take	rate	spade
bake	cave	state
came	gave	trade
fame	save	scale
game	wave	shape
lame	cane	shave
name	lane	blade
tame	mane	blaze
gale	case	chase
male	made	snake
sale	safe	grave
pale	bale	escape
tale	brave	mistake
date	flame	

Magic e with i

hide	nine	slide
ride	pine	glide
side	wine	swipe
tide	pipe	spine
wide	ripe	smile
life	wipe	prize
wife	bite	grime
bike	kite	chime
hike	dive	shine
like	five	white
mile	live	slime
pile	size	strike
tile	bride	stripe
time	spike	spider
dine	drive	tired
fine	crime	silent
line	tribe	vampire
mine	pride	

Magic e with o

bone	mole	coke	stole
cone	vole	tote	froze
tone	dole	pope	drove
home	joke	Rome	globe
dome	woke	alone	throne
dose	yoke	stone	stroke
nose	robe	broke	broken
hose	vote	spoke	explode
rose	note	choke	clothe
pose	rope	close	
doze	dope	scope	
pole	hope	those	
sole	code	slope	
hole	rode	smoke	

Magic with u

tube	super
cube	brute
tune	flute
cute	prune
use	plume
fuse	crude
rule	accuse
rude	excuse
mule	refuse
duke	
Luke	
fume	
huge	
June	

Vowel Digraph 'ai'

rain	bait	plain
main	aim	grain
pain	saint	drain
gain	quaint	train
vain	faint	Spain
pail	paint	brain
fail	painful	chain
mail	daisy	again
rail	raisin	snail
sail	afraid	frail
nail	obtain	claim
jail	explain	complain
tail	maintain	contain
paid	entertain	raid
maid	laid	strain
aid	waist	trail
wait	stain	

Vowel Digraph 'ea' as in 'heat'

eat	seam	easy
sea	mean	feast
seat	bean	gleam
beat	seal	greasy
meat	meal	least
heat	deal	reach
neat	lead	season
feat	beam	reason
heap	peak	scream
leap	cheat	stream
reap	speak	teach
weak	flea	treat
leak	steam	
beak	cream	
tea	clean	
leaf	dream	
team	each	

Vowel Digraph 'ea' as in 'head'

head	breadth
lead	ready
dead	deadly
read	steady
deaf	healthy
death	feather
bread	weather
sweat	heather
dread	leather
tread	sweater
spread	weapon
thread	instead
breast	meant
dreamt	heavy

Vowel Digraph 'ee'

bee	jeep	weed	bleep
see	peep	free	greed
deed	keep	tree	cheek
feed	deep	sleet	agree
eel	seem	fleet	between
need	peel	sweet	coffee
seed	feel	tweet	freezing
weed	reel	green	sheep
seek	heel	greet	sheet
week	seen	creep	sleek
leek	been	sleep	speed
feet	keen	steep	steel
meet	beef	sweep	teeth
weep	reed	bleed	three

Vowel Digraph 'er'

fern	butter	enter	camera	plaster	yesterday
kerb	after	ever	desert	river	winner
jerk	anger	faster	western	scatter	upper
herd	better	flutter	remember	several	proper
term	bigger	perch	hunter	shiver	number
jerkin	chatter	stern	gather	splinter	pepper
serpent	chopper	person	interested	summer	mutter
perfect	clever	permit	killer	winter	
servant	crosser	perhaps	letter	supper	
under	dagger	mineral	matter	temper	
over	deeper	interest	monster	thunder	
liver	dinner	deliver	never	together	

Vowel Digraph 'oa'

boat	hoax	moan	roast	soaking	boastful
goat	foal	road	coach	poacher	loaded
oak	foam	toad	float	groaning	bloated
coal	coat	goal	stoat	floating	
loaf	load	oath	cloak	cocoa	
soak	soap	boast	groan	loaves	
oats	loan	coast	croak	soapy	
Joan	roam	toast	throat	cockroach	

Vowel Digraph 'oo' as in 'moon'

food	moon	foolish	droop
mood	noon	oozing	gloom
tool	hoop	woosh	spoon
fool	hoof	afternoon	swoon
cool	doom	tooth	smooth
pool	roof	stool	snoop
boot	boom	shoot	groom
root	loom	croon	
loot	room	troop	
too	zoom	broom	
zoo	mood	proof	
soon	toot	swoop	

Vowel Digraph 'oo' as in 'book'

look	looking
took	cooking
cook	goodness
book	booking
rook	booked
nook	wool
hook	shook
foot	brook
soot	crook
hood	stood
good	blood
wood	flood

Vowel Digraph 'ow' as in 'cow'

how	prowler
now	rowing
row	downfall
vow	drowsy
cow	allowed
bow	however
wow!	clown
town	frown
down	brown
gown	crown
howl	drown
owl	crown
fowl	rowdy
flower	allow
shower	growl

Vowel Digraph 'ow' as in 'low'

low	shown	shadow	crowing
bow	flown	pillow	snowman
mow	grown	shallow	snowball
row	thrown	yellow	
tow	thrown	hollow	
own	bowler	barrow	
bowl	mower	elbow	
crow	growth	follow	
grow	owing	willow	
blow	rowing	narrow	
slow	slowly	sorrow	
flow	widow	arrow	
glow	window	below	
snow	fellow	borrow	
show	mellow	snowing	

Vowel Digraph 'ay'

day	stay	gangway
may	tray	holiday
say	pray	today
pay	bray	Monday
way	slay	Sunday
gay	crayon	subway
hay	stray	yesterday
bay	spray	
jay	away	
lay	dismay	
ray	delay	
clay	betray	
sway	relay	
play	display	

Vowel Digraph 'ou'

out	sprouts	around
pout	scout	found
loud	stout	amount
count	cloud	mound
mount	proud	wound
foul	ground	discount
our	flour	rounders
hour	aloud	counter
mouth	pouch	surround
south	hound	thousand
spout	pound	without
shout	sound	trousers
trout	round	
about	bound	

Vowel Digraph 'ar'

car	harp	card	arm	snarl	target
far	cart	target	star	start	arch
jar	dart	marvel	spark	spar	march
bar	part	garden	shark	chart	starch
tar	lard	pardon	smart	mustard	harsh
lark	yard	artist	start	Tarzan	carved
mark	hard	party	scarf	alarm	market
bark	dark	varnish	charm	carpet	
farm	park	art	sharp	darling	
harm	barn	ark	scar	lizard	

106

Vowel Digraph 'or'

or	torch	afford
for	north	effort
form	forth	horrific
ford	corner	inform
horn	scorn	morsel
torn	border	pitchfork
cord	morning	snoring
lord	forget	snorting
born	forgotten	snorted
corn	forget	stubborn
worn	order	torment
cork	organ	visitor
fork	record	story
stork	comfort	factory
sworn	hornet	memory
sport	cornet	glory
short	fortress	victory
storm	important	
thorn	ornament	

Vowel Digraph 'ur'

fur	bursting	murky
purr	turning	Saturday
burn	suburb	curving
curl	burning	gurgling
curb	turban	unfurl
turn	turnip	
hurt	turkey	
turf	murmur	
surf	curly	
burnt	absurd	
hurl	furnish	
spurs	burglar	
churn	urchin	
church	disturb	
burst	Thursday	
spurn	urgent	
murder	burden	
further	sunburn	
furthest	return	

Vowel Digraph 'aw'

saw	bawl	crawl	thaw	hawk	see-saw
raw	caw	shawl	flaw	lawn	squawk
jaw	draw	brawl	dawn	awful	outlaw
paw	straw	scrawl	yawn	frogspawn	
law	prawn	claw	fawn	jackdaw	

Vowel Digraph 'ir'

fir	birch	whirl	dirty	shirker	thirteen
sir	birth	twirl	thirsty	shirking	infirm
bird	mirth	shirk	thirst	chirping	birthday
girl	stir	chirp	firmly	stirring	firtree
dirt	skirt	squirm	firstly	twirling	blackbird
firm	shirt	squint	girder	confirm	
first	third	swirl	firmer	girlish	

Vowel Digraph 'ew'

new	grew	blew	screw	jewel	newest
dew	crew	stew	threw	newer	Andrew
pew	chew	flew	newt	fewer	Stewart
few	drew	brew	news	sewer	newspaper

APPENDICES

Examples of Testing and Recording

Appendix 1 includes examples of tests for assessing children's phonic knowledge and record sheets which have been developed by two Midlands primary schools. Both schools encourage a systematic approach to the teaching of phonics as part of a proactive reading policy. The sample pages reproduced here are intended to act as a stimulus to other schools who wish to develop their own assessment procedures.

Please note that these examples of tests and record sheets are copyright. They must not be copied or reproduced in any way without prior permission having been obtained.

Appendix 1 (a)
Corngreaves Primary School, Sandwell, West Midlands

Previously, the school had used the *Phonic Skills Tests* (Jackson) but teachers found them time-consuming. The need to assess and record phonic skills was recognised, therefore, the school developed its own tests with fewer items.

Altogether, there are eight Phonic Tests: Letters; C-V-C Blending; Consonant Digraphs; Initial Consonant Blends; Final Consonant Blends; Magic 'e'; Long Consonant Digraphs; and Vowel Digraphs.

The school commences the recording process at the end of Reception Year, by which time the children will have benefited from a year of instruction using *Letterland*. The records follow each child through the school but are discontinued when it is felt that his or her phonics are secure.

Records are updated termly. Additional assessment, using the tests, may be undertaken for a specific reason, for example to gather information before a meeting with parents, referral to the Child Psychology Service, or before being discussed by the school's SEN Discussion Group. Records are always updated at the end of the school year, in readiness for the child's new class and teacher.

Testing and Recording Procedures

1. So that there is no need to date entries on the record sheets, use different coloured inks for each year group: Year R/1 – blue; Year 2 – red; Year 3 – black; Year 4+ – green.
2. Allow six seconds for word building.
3. Leave a minimum of one month before re-testing to ensure that learning is permanent.
4. Allow two errors on each test, except for Test 1 (Letters of the Alphabet - not included here as an example), where there must be no errors.
5. Fill in the record sheet after each test has been completed successfully.
6. Use the supplementary comment sheet where appropriate.

Phonic Test 3 - Cons. Digraphs

whip	chip	when	this	chop
shed	graph	shop	mash	path
witch	bunch	rich	that	dash
phone	flush	shelf	sash	tenth
while	whisk	maths	chap	chess
itch	lunch	thank	rush	why
crash	then	bench	what	photo

Phonic Test 6 - 'Magic e'

tape	home	mile	note	cute
rule	same	nose	hate	like
lime	joke	nice	bake	fuse
these	bone	mute	eve	cope
note	kite	hose	make	use
gaze	fire	bite	gate	yoke
tide	page	mule	cave	rude

Phonic Test 8 - Vowel Digraphs

cow	foe	dart	new	out

raw	cue	hood	term	ray

low	tied	deaf	jeep	burn

coat	haul	gain	boy	bird

heap	soon	sort	coil	loud

jerk	lied	bowl	horn	hurt

sail	paw	sir	need	due

TEL. 0151 231 5216/5299

Appendix 1 (b)
Blackheath Primary School, Sandwell, West Midlands

The phonic record sheets are used both for assessment and record keeping, starting in the Reception Year. They are written in the same typeface as the childrens' reading books. Nonsense words are used to ensure that phonic skills are being used and avoid the possibility of the child using word recognition. Tests are repeated after four to five weeks to check that the learning is permanent. The records are kept in the childrens' files and follow them through the school.

Phonic Checklist 1 - Letters

Name | **D.O.B.**

1. Recognition of Letter.
2. Knowledge of Sound.
3. Knowledge of Letter Name.

Phonic Test 1

Letter	1	2	3
l			
i			
h			
n			
y			
c			
w			
m			
s			
b			
d			
a			
r			

Letter	1	2	3
f			
p			
g			
j			
t			
u			
o			
k			
e			
q			
v			
x			
z			

Blackheath Primary School
Phonic Skills Record

Name

Sheet 4
Blending

	Date	Date	Date
rik			
wap			
han			
gup			
zin			
mox			
gup			
rud			
waf			
div			
hef			
tox			
dum			

	Date	Date	Date
sog			
fod			
mal			
neg			
peb			
dob			
vas			
pof			
yeg			
gol			
lig			
jun			
caz			

Date Completed

Blackheath Primary School
Phonic Skills Record

Name

	Date	Date	Date
shob			
chan			
mich			
thag			
whep			
dech			
thun			
shud			
chup			
dith			
shom			
luch			
shid			

	Date	Date	Date
chen			
kesh			
huth			
lesh			
shib			
chog			
chob			
chid			
pash			
whum			
thim			
lesh			
peth			

Date Completed

115

Blackheath Primary School
Phonic Skills Record

Name

Sheet 6
Magic e

	Date	Date	Date
lope			
pebe			
dube			
cale			
cobe			
lote			
hipe			
beze			
deke			
bule			
kole			
hile			
pibe			

	Date	Date	Date
hene			
naze			
pabe			
tude			
kine			
nebe			
lape			
moke			
hume			
dape			
hame			
muke			
pite			

Date Completed

116

Phonic Checklist 2-8 - Word Building

| Name | | D.O.B. | |

C-V-C (Short Vowel)

Phonic Test 2

a			
e			
i			
o			
u			

Consonant Digraphs

Phonic Test 3

sh			
ch			
th			
wh			
ph			

'Magic e'

Phonic Test 6

a-e			
i-e			
o-e			
o-u			

Initial Cons. Blends

Phonic Test 4

Final Cons. Blends

Phonic Test 5

Vowel Digraphs

Phonic Test 8

Long Cons. Digraphs

Phonic Test 7

© Blackheath Primary School, Sandwell.

Blackheath Primary School
Phonic Skills Record

Summary Sheet

Name [ ]

Letterland Characters [ ]

Letter Sounds [ ]

Letter Names [ ]

C-V-C Blending [ ]

Consonant Digraphs [ ]

Magic e [ ]

Supplementary Comments Sheet

Add details which are not included on tests or record sheets e.g. b-d confusion

Name	D.O.B.

Test No.

Test No.

Test No.

Test No.

Appendix 2
Sandwell Group Phonic Tests - Answers
Trial Version

Test 1:

1. if	2. an	3. on	4. it
5. us	6. pat	7. egg	8. cup
9. got	10. van	11. sum	12. leg
13. rid	14. din	15. tub	16. bet
17. mad	18. wed	19. nut	20. hot
21. gap	22. kit	23. zip	24. jam	25. fix

Test 2:

1. camp	2. cost	3. rink	4. halt	5. mend
6. wasp	7. mint	8. hang	9. risk	10. gulp
11. bold	12. sift	13. rude	14. wave	15. dive
16. cone	17. eve	18. plan	19. frog	20. drum
21. prop	22. trod	23. skin	24. crop	25. brim
26. snap	27. clam	28. grip	29. glad	30. span
31. flat	32. blot	33. swam	34. smug	35. scab
36. star	37. quit	38. slip	39. twin	40. supper
41. bitter	42. filler	43. ladder	44. funny	45. wicker
46. hammer	47. lesson	48. shot	49. chin	50. whip

Sandwell Group Phonic Test 1

School: ...Brightview Primary................................. Class: ....2..........

Name: .....Andrew.. Date ....:...:...92.....

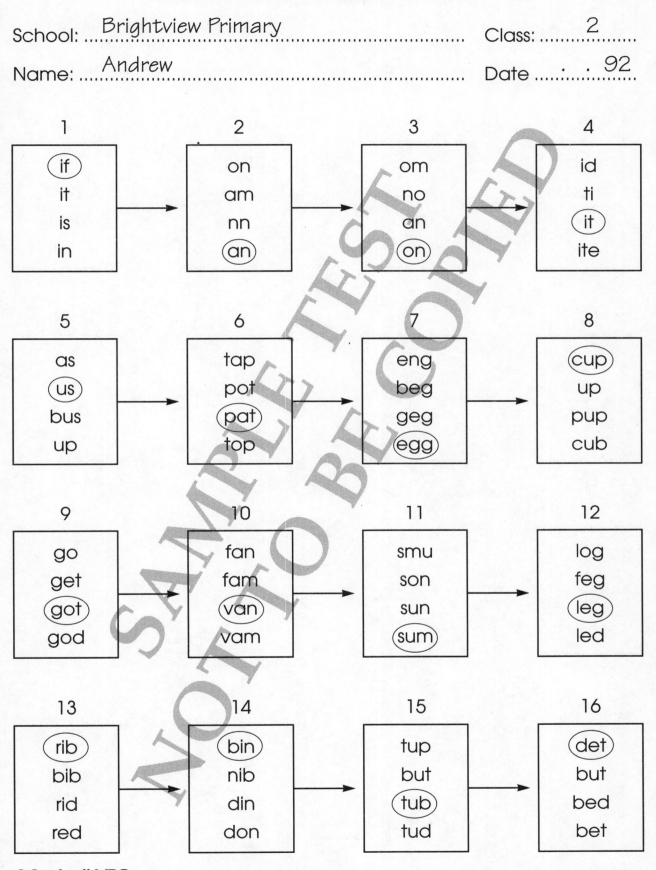

© Sandwell MBC.

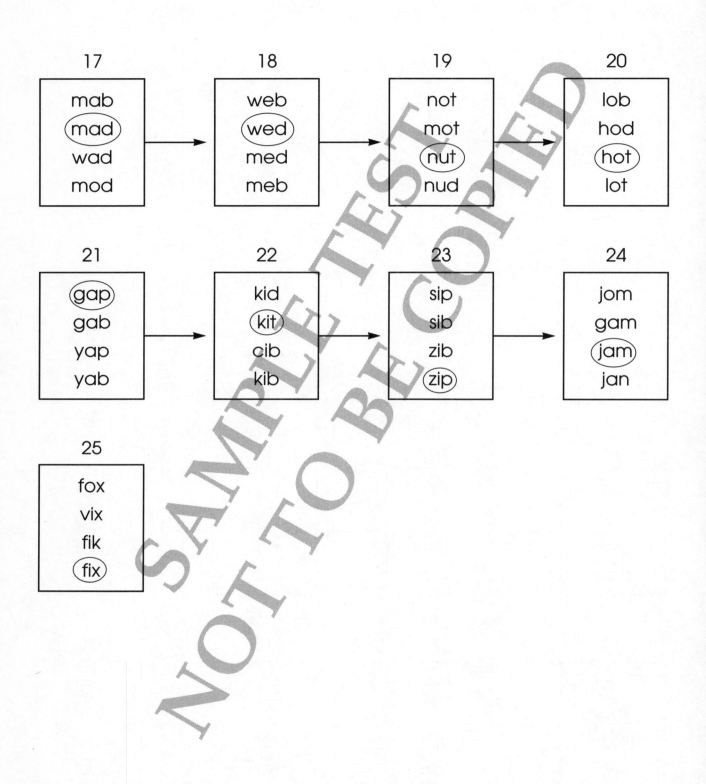

17

mab
(mad)
wad
mod

18

web
(wed)
med
meb

19

not
mot
(nut)
nud

20

lob
hod
(hot)
lot

21

(gap)
gab
yap
yab

22

kid
(kit)
cib
kib

23

sip
sib
zib
(zip)

24

jom
gam
(jam)
jan

25

fox
vix
fik
(fix)

Sandwell Group Phonic Test 2

School: ...Brightview Primary............................ Class: ......2......

Name: ...Andrew.. Date: ....:...:..92

1	2	3	4	5
cap	cots	rink	(haut)	mede
canp	(cost)	(rik)	hate	merd
(camp)	coct	rice	halt	(mend)
capm	cote	krin	hatt	medd

6	7	8	9	10
wasp	mind	hag	rike	(gup)
(waps)	(mint)	han	rise	gulp
swap	mitn	(hang)	rick	gupe
wap	mite	hagn	(risk)	grup

11	12	13	14	15
bolt	(sive)	rueb	woav	diy
boil	sife	(rud)	(wav)	diov
(bold)	sivd	rude	wave	dive
bode	sift	read	waf	(div)

16	17	18	19	20
cone	ethe	blan	flog	(brum)
con	eve	pan	(frog)	durm
(ceon)	(hef)	(plan)	fog	drum
coin	elf	pane	foge	dum

21	22	23	24	25
brap	tod	(sink)	cop	birm
(prop)	(trod)	sin	crop	brim
pop	tord	sine	(corp)	bim
porp	tode	skin	proc	(drim)

26
(snap)
pans
sanp
span

27
calm
(clam)
cam
came

28
gipe
glip
(grip)
gip

29
grad
gad
(gald)
glad

30
san
span
(snap)
sanp

31
falt
(flat)
fatl
fate

32
(bot)
blot
botl
bolt

33
(smaw)
sam
swam
samw

34
(sug)
smug
sumg
stug

35
sab
spab
slab
(scab)

36
sar
srat
(star)
sare

37
(qiuf)
qait
quit
qoit

38
spil
slip
(sip)
sipe

39
(tin)
twin
tein
tuin

40
(super)
supper
sumper
sper

41
(biter)
bitter
bieter
beeter

42
feler
filer
(filr)
filler

43
larder
lader
laeder
(ladder)

44
funey
(funy)
funny
fueny

45
wiker
wicker
(wikr)
wieker

46
hammer
hamper
(hamer)
hemer

47
leson
leshon
(lesson)
leseon

48
shot
(slot)
soot
sot

49
shin
(chin)
cein
cin

50
(wip)
wipe
whip
wipp

Sandwell Group Phonic Tests Record Sheet

School: .....Brightview Primary..................... Class: ......2......

Teacher: ...Mrs. B... Date .....:....92

Name	Test Results			Skills to be taught/prc
	1	2	3	
Andrew			\	Practice of final consonant blends revision of initial consonant blends teach 'magic e'.

Appendix 3
Miscue Analysis

A miscue analysis is an observation of strategies and patterns used by the reader when reading a text aloud.

Carrying out a miscue analysis

The following preparations need to be made:

1. The selection of an appropriate section of text – a meaningful passage sufficiently difficult to generate at least 25 miscues. The stilted, repetitive prose of the early books of many graded reading schemes would not be suitable for this purpose.

2. The availability of an exact copy of the passage to enable the teacher to record the miscues.

3. The use of a tape recorder is advisable, at least for an inexperienced assesser. Thus, taped readings by the pupil can be replayed several times to ensure accuracy in coding and recording, thus improving the likelihood of a detailed and perceptive analysis. For the busy teacher, recording the reading enables the coding and recording to be made at a later, and perhaps more convenient, time.

Recording Miscues

Type of Error	Code Used	Example
Substitution	Underline and write in substituted word.	The crow <u>was</u> pleased. *(were)*
Refusal	Dotted line under the word.	The crow was p̲l̲e̲a̲s̲e̲d̲.
Insertion	Use ʌ and write in additional words used.	The crow was ʌ pleased. *(very)*
Omission	Circle any word(s) included in text but not read.	You are a (very) beautiful bird.
Pause	Use the symbol | when the pause is more than 3 seconds.	You are a very | beautiful bird.
Teacher assistance given (to maintain fluency and meaning)	Use letters TA near word. Normally preceded by | ('pause' code).	… make the | changes TA.
Repetition	Identify repeated words with a curved line.	You are a very beautiful bird.
Correction	Write in initial miscue and add a © if corrected by the reader.	You are a very beautiful <u>bird</u>. © *(boy)*

Tina's Reading

We cannot see the air, but the

changes in the air around us make

the|changes in our weather. These [There's]

changes are far [for] too big and far [for] too

strong for anyone to stop.

From [for] outer space the swirling clouds [colds]

look weak [wek] and gentle. [gets] |however,

men are really rather small TA

creatures, and storms and floods, [frogs]

gales [glass] and dry weather may mean life

and [or] death to us.

So [Some] people have to learn [lean] to live with

the weather. [water] We must keep

ourselves warm, our homes ©

comfortable, and our journeys [jobs] safer,

whatever weather comes. TA

People know more about the

weather now then they have ever

known before. [now] there are always

|satellites spinning round the world

|sending back pictures of the clouds [clubs] TA

as they are seen from [for] outer [other] space. [spack]

128

Analysis of Tina's Miscues

Tina appears to have developed a reasonable sight vocabulary. There is evidence that Tina is following much of the meaning of the text and makes substitutions which fit into their context, eg 'or' for 'and' (line 11) and 'some' for 'so' (line 12).

The error in line 2 suggests that Tina is not skilled in using forward-acting cues (reading ahead in a search for meaning), particularly when reading to the next line is required.

Phonically, Tina has mastered letter sounds; most of her substitutions commencing with the correct consonantal sound.

An appropriate programme for phonic skills for Tina would appear to be:

1. A revision of modified vowels, 'ar', 'er', 'ir' 'or' and 'ur', with particular emphasis on 'ar'.

2. Work on initial consonant blends.

3. Work on the Magic 'e' rule.

This would form an initial programme. On completion, a second analysis could be carried out, both to confirm the success of the teaching to date and to determine whether the remaining difficulties still persist. A different passage for the reassessment should be selected; the text of which should include words containing the phonic elements still needing attention, ie soft 'c', soft 'g' and vowel digraph 'ea'.

A single miscue may be open to more than one interpretation which emphasises the necessity of choosing a passage of sufficient length and selectivity to provide sufficient examples. Thus, Tina's reading of 'clubs' for 'clouds' could be interpreted either as a b-d confusion or as a word with initial letters which suggested a 'meaningful' substitution. The correct use of the initial consonant blend suggests that Tina may be starting to master such blends. It would therefore follow that a specific check of initial consonant blends would be helpful in determining whether there was a need for revision or teaching in those skills.

Appendix 4
Probe Sheet 1
Say b f s m a
38/40 on two consecutive occasions

b	f	s	m	a	5
a	m	b	s	f	10
m	a	s	f	b	15
f	b	a	s	m	20
a	s	m	b	f	25
b	m	f	a	s	30
a	s	b	m	f	35
s	m	f	b	a	40